Japanese Grammar 101

No Boring Linguistic Jargon
No Overly Complex Explanations

The Easy To Digest, Simple
Approach to Japanese

© Copyright 2017 - All rights reserved.

By

Languages World

© **Copyright 2017 - All rights reserved .**

The contents of this book may not be reproduced, duplicated or transmitted without direct written permission from the author.

Under no circumstances will any legal responsibility or blame be held against the publisher for any reparation, damages, or monetary loss due to the information herein, either directly or indirectly.

Legal Notice:

This book is copyright protected. This is only for personal use. You cannot amend, distribute, sell, use, quote or paraphrase any part or the content within this book without the consent of the author.

Disclaimer Notice:

Please note the information contained within this document is for educational and entertainment purposes only. Every attempt has been made to provide accurate, up to date and reliable complete information. No warranties of any kind are expressed or implied. Readers acknowledge that the author is not engaging in the rendering of legal, financial, medical or professional advice. The content of this book has been derived from various sources.

Contents

Introduction はじめに 6

Politeness Levels 敬語の使い分け（尊敬語/丁寧語/謙譲語） 10

Pronunciation 発音 12

The Basics 基本 15

Introductions 紹介の仕方 24

Pronouns 代名詞 31

Demonstratives (ko-so-a-do) 指示語-（こ・そ・あ・ど） 35

Super Simple Structure とても基本的な文章構造 44

Desu Conjugation です活用形 50

Possessive Pronouns 所有代名詞 57

Like / Dislike 好き/好きじゃない 63

Question Marker "ka" クエスチョンマーク"か" 67

Question Word: Whose? 疑問形:誰の 72

Adjectives 形容詞 74

I Adjective Conjugation い形容詞活用形 79

Na Adjective Conjugation な形容詞活用形 86

Number in Japanese 日本語の数字 92

Question Word: How Much? 質問形:どれくらい 96

Japanese Verbs 日本語の動詞 99

Masu Verb Conjugation ます動詞活用形 104

Informal Verb Conjugation 敬語でない動詞の活用形 115

Future Tense & Time Expression 未来形と時間表現 119

Particles 助詞 125

Wh- Questions 質問形 134

Japanese Sentence Structure 日本語の文章構造 138

Expressing Desire 欲求表現 144

Want to – Tai Form たい活用形 148

Frequency Words 頻度を表す単語 154

Inviting お誘い 156

Te-form て一活用形 160

Present Continuous Form 現在継続の表し方 165

I Have 私は持っています 172

Existence - There is/ There are 存在一がある 178

Making Requests 依頼 184

Asking For Permission 許可を得る 187

Expressing too much 過剰表現 191

Counters 数え方 197

Ordering 注文 200

Masho – let's ましょう 205

More than 比較級—より 209

The Most 最上級 215

Have you ever?—ことがありますか 218

Connecting Verbs 動詞のつなぎ方 222

Connecting Adjectives 形容詞のつなぎ方 225

Telling Time in Japanese 日本語での時間の伝え方
.... 229

Time & Distance 時間と距離 233

Conclusion 239

Introduction はじめに

Welcome to Japanese Grammar 101! Grammar is the central pillar of language learning, however many students struggle learning it. New language structures, different tenses and conjugation can be intimidating.

We've heard lines like "grammar sucks", "I hate grammar" and we can understand why.
Most books out there teach grammar in a overly grammary way, that just flys over your head. There is nothing worse than being taught a new language only to be constantly stuck and confused. We don't want this!

Learning grammar shouldn't be a struggle, and a big reason why new students give up, is from being overwhelmed. When you don't understand something, making progress is near impossible. If you've picked this book up, you're commited to improving your Japanaese grammar, so that's a great step in the right direction.

In this book we aim to overcome these problems, by teaching you grammar that focuses on giving you results – instead of getting you bored. We'll walk alongside you, so you don't get confused. No linguistic jargon that you will hardly ever use or overly complex explainations. Instead a practical approach to Japanese that will keep you wanting to learn, more and more.

So whether you are learning for business, travel or to make new friends. You can make Japanese grammar click.

About this book
This book is designed for beginner level speakers. No hard to digest sections that are difficult to understand, only bit size learning that you can manage – promise!
We aim to give you a solid grammar foundation that you can build upon. Therefore each section is based on a specific topic that builds on the previous. After each topic there will be a short exercise to test how well you have understood the section.

You may come across topics that you don't feel like skipping however stick to them, they'll become essential later in the book.

Follow these step by step and you'll be speaking Japanese in no time. And by the end of this series you'll be able to communicate with people in Japanese like never before. Trust me you'll be amazed at your results.

Grammar Learning Tips
1. Write in this book
This book is yours for life, feel free to scribble down notes and key points to remember – in fact we recommend it. Writing notes helps with long term memory and puts you in the zone, allowing everything to sink in better. Plus it's great for reference.

2. Patience equals Fluency
Many learners are so eager to learn. They rush through sections, hoping to absorb the language fast. Instead of learning quickly, they end up getting overwhelmed twice as fast. Don't fall in this trap, each section of this book is designed to build on top of the previous. Take it easy and make sure you fully understand each topic before moving on. There's no rush, learning a language takes time!

3. You don't have to know it all

We cover a lot of topics in this book, you don't need to know all of them to begin speaking Japanese. From the start you'll be learning useful phrases and structures. So we recommend, once you've studied a few sections, start putting them into practice. Don't wait until you've finished the book, learn as you go, bit by bit.

I think we've covered enough of the ground work, now let's begin learning Japanese!

Politeness Levels
敬語の使い分け (尊敬語/丁寧語/謙譲語)

One of the main parts of Japanese that's confusing as an English speaker, is politeness levels. In Japanese society politeness levels are very important to show respect and avoid being rude.

There are three types of politeness levels in Japanese:
- Informal speech
  Spoken with family and close friends

- Formal speech
  Spoken with strangers and colleagues

- Very fromal speech
  Spoken with teachers, bosses and customers

Using the incorrect politeness level is not the end of the world, however if possible, you should try and use the correct one.

Learning all three politeness levels can be very overwhelming. So we recommend to start with formal speech, as you can use this for most situations. Once you have the basics of formal speech down, using casual speech will become easier. Very formal speech is more advanced, so in this book we will be covering the informal and formal speech. These will be marked with the following:

Legend
(f) = formal speech
(inf) = informal speech

Pronunciation 発音

Japanese pronunciation can be a tricky to understand, so we want to cover it in this first section.

A common mistake new learner's make is trying to pronounce Japanese characters the same was as in English. Although some character sounds remain the same, a lot are very different. So it's a good idea to get familiar with these pronunciations before you begin learning Japanese.

Vowels
Vowel in Japanese sound different to English. Have a look at the table below and practice speaking the listed words so you can get familiar with the sounds used.

Vowel	Sound	Example
a	ah as in art	akura
e	eh as in bed	eki
i	ee as in see	ichi
o	oh as in coat	odoru
u	oo as in moo	uma

Let's see the pronunciation break down

Akura =   ah-koo-rah
Eki   =   eh-kee
Ichi   =   ee-chee
Odoru =   oh-doh-roo
Uma   =   oo-mah

Double vowels

Double vowels lengthen the sound in Japanese, sometimes these are represented with a dash on top of the vowel.

Vowel	Sound	Example
aa	a as in father	okaasan
ee	e as in den	oneesan
ii	ee as in see	iiau
oo	oh as in coat	omou
uu	oo as in moo	fuun

Pronunciation breakdown:
okaasan   =   oh-kaa-sahn
oneesan   =   oh-nee-sahn
iiau   =   ee-ahoo
omou   =   oh-moou
fuun   =   f-oon

Keep an eye out for double vowels as meanings of words can change based on stress on the vowel:

ie   =   house
iie   =   no

Obasan   =   aunt
Obaasan   =   grandmother

Double Consonants
Whenever we have two consonants together, we need to put more stress on that character.

Gakko   = school
Kitte   = postal stamp
Rokku = six

Double constants meanings can also change depending on the stress applied. So make sure you look out for these aswell.

The Basics 基本

Moving onto some basics, the first thing you will need to know in any language is how to greet someone.

Good morning (f)
= 	Ohayo gozaimasu おはようございます

Good afternoon
= 	Konbanwa こんばんは

Hello
= 	konnichiwa こんにちは

Goodbye (f)
= 	Sayounara さようなら

How are you?
= 	Ogenki desu ka? お元気ですか

I'm fine
= 	Genki desu 元気です

I'm not okay
= 	Genki ja arimasen 元気じゃありません

So so
=	Maa maa desu まあまあです

For informal speech, "Konnichiwa こんにちは" and "Konbanwa こんばんは" are not used, especially among friends. Instead, we call a person by their name, or simply say "Hai はい" similar to 'Hi こんにちは' in English.
Here are some examples for casual greetings.

Good Morning (inf)
=	Ohayo おはよう

See you (inf)
=	Jyaa (ne) じゃあ（ね）/ Bai bai ばいばい

How are you? (inf)
=	Genki? 元気

I'm fine (inf)
=	Genki 元気

I'm not fine (inf)
=	Genki janai 元気じゃない

So so (inf)
=	Maa maa まあまあ

When talking with people you know, it's more common to ask them specific things rather than simply saying "How are you" (genki desu ka 元気ですか)

To do this we can use the following pattern

Noun + wa+ do desu ka?
名詞 + は + どうですか
How is …. ?

Let's see some examples:

How is work?
= Shigoto wa do desu ka?
仕事はどうですか
(How is/are = do desu ka? どうですか)
(Work = Shigoto 仕事)

How is school?
= Gakko wa do desu ka?
学校はどうですか
(How is/are = do desu ka? どうですか)
(School = Gakko 学校)

In informal speech, we leave out "desu ka ですか"

Example
How is work? (inf)
= Shigoto wa do?
仕事はどうですか
(How is/are = do? どう)
(Work = Shigoto 仕事)

However this speech is used more with family and friends.

Topic particle "wa は"
In the above sentence structure we use the topic particle "wa は". Particles are used to modify a meaning of a word. As you learn more about Japanese, you will notice more and more particles.

This particle in placed right after the topic of the sentence. And tells the listener what the sentence is about.

We can translate this to "as for" "speaking of…."

Examples
I am tired
(as for me) I am tired

Watashi wa tsukare teru
私は 疲れてる
(watashi 私= I) (tired = tsukare teru 疲れてる)

Where is your hometown?
(as for) your hometown where is it?
Shusshin wa doko desu ka?
出身はどこですか
(hometown = shusshin 出身)
(where is it = doko desu ka? どこですか)

Wa は is one of the most used particles when speaking japanese. Just remember it is used to mark a topic.

Basic Greeting
Now let's put what we have learnt together and go through a basic Japanese greeting.

Sato: Ohayo Gozaimasu

おはようございます

(Good morning)

Tanaka: Ohayo Gozaimasu

おはようございます

(Good morning)

Genki desu ka? げんきですか

(How are you?)

Sato: Hai, Genki desu はい、元気です

(I'm fine.)

Tanaka san, shigoto wa do desu ka?
田中さん、仕事はどうですか

(Mr. Tanaka, how is your work?)

Tanaka: Shigoto wa juncho desu
仕事は順調です

(Work goes well.)

Sato: Sayonara さようなら

(Bye bye)

This is a formal greeting, if you want to make an informal greeting, simply use the casual words stated in the previous section.

Suffix "san さん"

Something you may have noticed in the conversation is the use of the word "san さん". "san さん" is used after a name to shows politeness or respect.

"san さん" can be used for both men and women, to a family name or first name.

    Mr. / Mrs. / Ms. Sato   = **Sato san**

    Yumi (girl's first name)   = **Yumi san**

    Takeshi (boy's first name)   = **Takeshi san**

When talking to people who are the same age or younger we use different suffixes:

We use:
"chan ちゃん" for girls
"kun くん" for boys

For example:
Yumi **chan**
Takeshi **kun**

Exercise
Highlight the topic of these sentences:

1) I am a student
2) Your dog is cute
3) I am going to the park this weekend
4) Suzuki watched tv at home

Answers
1) I am a student
Topic = I
(as for) I, am student

2) Your dog is cute
Topic = your dog
(as for) your dog, is cute

3) I am going to the park this weekend
Topic = weekend
(as for) weekend, I am going to the park

4) Suzuki watched tv at home
Topic = Suzuki
(as for) Suzuki, watched tv at home

Introductions 紹介の仕方

Now let's cover some self-introductions.
When stating your name there are two ways to do this:

My name is ...
=	Watashi no namae wa + **(name)** + desu
=	私の名前は+ **(name)** +です

Or

I am ...
=	Watashi wa + **(name)** + desu
=	私は + **(name)** + です

(**I** = Watashi 私)
(**Name** = Namae 名前)

When using the phrase: **Watashi no namae** 私の名前: "no の" is a particle to show possession. In this sentences it is used to state "the name belongs to me".

The use of particle "no の" will be explained in a later section. For now just remember "watashi no namae" as a set phrase and don't analyse it too much.

"desu です" is used in place of – is, am, are
We will also cover this in depth later.

Example
I am Toyota
Watashi no namae wa Toyota desu
私の名前は豊田です

Or

Watashi wa Toyota desu
私は豊田です

How to ask about someone's name
To ask someone what his/her name is, we use this phrase:

What is your name?
=	Onamae wa nan desu ka?
    お名前はなんですか

You can omit "nan desu ka なんですか" (what is?") and ask simply "onamae wa お名前は" but this more informal.

Your name is? (inf)
=   Onamae wa? お名前は

Now, to ask where he/she is from:

Where are you from?
=   Susshin wa doko desu ka?
         出身はどこですか

Or, informally:

Where are you from? (inf)
=   Shusshin wa? 出身は

Shusshin actually translates to hometown. The literal translation is "where is your hometown?"

To answer we use this phrase:

I am from England
=   Igirisu shusshin desu
         イギリス出身です

         (or simplified)

=   Igirisu desu
         イギリスです

(England = Igirisu イギリス)

Again, here the literal translation is "England is my hometown"
Next, to say "nice to meet you" in Japanese:

Nice to meet you / you too
=	Yoroshiku onegai shimasu
よろしくお願いします

You too (alternative)
=	Kochira koso こちらこそ

"Yoroshiku onegai shimasu よろしくお願いします" can also be used in other situation because it also translates to "I am looking forward to working with you", however this is for business situations.

In the previous section we learnt "genki desu ka 元気ですか?" is used to ask "how are you". But in Japanese you might find someone saying "hajimemashite はじめまして" when they first meet you.

How do you do?
=	Hajimemashite
はじめまして

The phrase "Hajimemashite はじめまして" is often translated as "Nice to meet you" or "How do you do" in English.

This phrase is only used with people you have never met before. Therefore it is a first time greeting with strangers. After you have met the person and cannot say "hajimemashite はじめまして", instead you would say "genki desu ka 元気ですか".

Basic Conversation - part II
Now, let's put these phrases together and go through a basic introduction in Japanese.

Yoshida: Hajimemashite はじめまして
(How do you do?)

Toyota: Konnichiwa, Hajimemashite
にちは、はじめまして
(Hello, how do you do?)

Yoshida: Watashi no namae wa Yoshida desu. Onamae wa?
私の名前は吉田です。お名前は
(My name is Yoshida. And your name?)

Toyota: Toyota desu. 豊田です
(I am Toyota.)

Yoshida: Shusshin wa doko desu ka?
出身はどこですか
(Where are you from?)

Toyota: Tokyo shusshin desu. Yoshida san wa?
東京出身です。吉田さんは
(I'm from Tokyo. What about you, Mr. Yoshida?)

Yoshida: Osaka shusshin desu.
大阪出身です
(I'm from Osaka.)

Toyota: So desu ka. Yorosiku onegai shimasu
そうですか。よろしくお願いします
(I see. Nice to meet you.)
[I see = so desu ka そうですか]

Yoshida: Kochirakoso yoroshiku onegai shimau
こちらこそよろしくお願いします
(You too.)

28

Pronouns 代名詞

Now that we understand basic introductions, let's move onto covering personal subject pronouns. Simply put, it refers to words like: I, you, he etc.

I	=	Watashi 私
	=	Boku/Ore 僕/俺 (masculine, inf)
You	=	Anata あなた
You (plural)	=	Anatagata あなた方 (f) Anata tachi あなた達 (inf)
He	=	Kare 彼
She	=	Kanojo 彼女
We	=	Watashi tachi 私達
They	=	Karera 彼ら

The pronouns for "he" and "she" are also used to mean "boyfriend" and "girlfriend" in Japanese, so keep an eye out for these.

In Japanese personal pronouns are rarely used when speaking. Instead we use the person's name:

~~She~~ is cute
~~Kanojo~~ wa kawaii
~~彼女~~はかわいい
=
Kim is cute
Kim san wa kawaii desu
キムさんはかわいいです

~~You~~ are tall
Miko (you) are tall
Miko san wa segatakai desu
みこさんは背が高いです

If we don't know the person's name, then we have to use these pronouns. However if you do know, it should be avoided.

Common beginner mistake
Many beginners, over use the word "watashi 私". Japanese speakers find this very annoying.

In English we use 'I' pronoun a lot. However in Japanese "watashi" is dropped when it is clear we are talking about ourselves.

For example, if you have already said "watashi wa 私は" and the conversation topic is still on you. You no longer need to use "watashi wa 私は".

Examples
Watashi wa John desu 私はジョンです
~~Watashi wa~~ Isha desu
私は医者です
(doctor = isha 医者)

In this example we can just say "isha desu 医者です" as it's already clear we are still talking about ourselves.

Once the topic changes, then we can use "watashi wa 私は" again to bring the topic back to ourselves.

This can be applied to any topic we are talking about, if the topic of the conversation is still the same.

Examples
Japanese food is cheap

Nipponshoku wa yasui
日本食は安い

Japanese food is healthy
~~Nipponshoku wa~~ oishī desu
~~日本食は~~おいしいです

Demonstratives (ko-so-a-do)
指示語-(こ・ そ・ あ・ ど)

Demonstratives refers to words, such as "this", "that", "here", "there", etc

Japanese demonstratives are very different to English. They follow the pattern ko-so-a-do. However for each case the final letters change depending on what you want to express.
Let's go through them one by one.

Unspecific demonstratives

Japanese unspecific demonstratives are followed by the letters "re" after each ko-so-a-do. The reason they're unspecific is because they do not refer to any particular noun.
The forms are:

"kore これ", "sore それ", "are あれ", "dore どれ"

Each of these demonstratives are used according to the distance of an object from both the speaker and listener.

Kore これ (this)	Close to the speaker Far from the listener
Sore それ(that)	Far from the speaker Close to the listener
Are あれ (that)	Far from both speaker and listener
Dore? どれ	(Which one?)

Therefore when using unspecific demonstratives you have to judge how close an object is to you.

Let's see how this would work in a real life situation.

At a restaurant:
I want to talk about the food I've been served. In this case we would use "kore これ" because the food I'm talking about is closer to me than the listener.

I want to talk about food my friend's been served, I would use "sore それ" because it's closer to my friend than me.

I want to talk about something that is far from both of us, for example the outside of the restaurant, I would use "are あれ".

I want to ask, "which one is tasty" I would use "dore どれ":

For example
What is this?
Kore wa nan desu ka?
これはなんですか
(what = nan なん)

That is a sushi
Sore wa sushi desu
それは寿司です

Specific demonstratives

If we want to be specific about an item, we use the ending "no" after each ko-so-a-do word.

These word follow the same distance pattern as "kore これ", "sore それ", "are あれ" "dore どれ" .

Kono この **(this + noun)**   Close to the speaker

	Far from the listener
Sono その **(that + noun)**	Far from the speaker Close to the listener
Ano あの **(that + noun)**	Far from both speaker and listener
Dono? どの	Which (noun)

Examples
Kono Pasokon
このパソコン
= **This PC**
(pasokon = pc)

Sono Pasokon
そのパソコン
= **That PC**
(close to the listener, far from the speaker)

Ano Pasokon
あのパソコン
= **That PC**
(far from both listener and speaker)

Dono Pasokon?
どのパソコン
=   **Which PC?**

From the examples you can see all demonstratives refer to a specific noun, therefore we have to use "kono この, sono その, ano あの, dono どの" and not "kore これ, sore それ, are あれ, dore どれ"

Location Demonstratives

If we want to talk about location, we can use demonstratives with the ending "ko"
These words follow the same distance pattern as "kore これ", "sore それ", "are あれ" "dore どれ"
.

Koko ここ **(here)**   Close to the speaker
                       Far from the listener

Soko そこ **(there)**   Close to the listener
                       Far from the speaker

Asoko あそこ **(there)**   Far from both
                           speaker and listener

Doko どこ **(where)**   Location unknown

Examples

The cat is here
Neko wa **koko** ni imasu
猫はここにいます
(cat = neko 猫)

The cat is there
Neko wa **soko** ni imasu
猫はそこにいます
(close to the listener, far from the speaker)

The cat is there
Neko wa **asoko** ni imasu
猫はあそこにいます
(far from both speaker and listener)

Where is the cat?
Neko wa **doko** desu ka?
猫はどこですか

The way we use these demonstratives in sentences will become clear once we reach the existence section.

Direction Demonstratives

When talking about directions, we can use demonstratives with the ending "chira"
These words follow the same distance pattern as "kore これ", "sore それ", "are あれ" "dore どれ".

Kochira こちら   Close to the speaker
(this way)   Far from the listener

Sochira そちら   Close to the listener
(that way)   Far from the speaker

Achira あちら   Far from both speaker and listener
(that way over there)

Dochira どちら   Which way?

In Japanese we normally use this pattern when introducing people. Referring to people as "this" or "that" is seen as being rude. Instead we use "this way" and "that way" which is more polite:

This is Akira
<u>Kochira</u> wa Akira desu
<u>こちら</u>は明です。

This way is Akira

Who is that person? (over there)
Achira wa donata desu ka?
明はどなたですか

There are more forms of ko-so-a-do words in Japanese but they are more advanced. These are the most common you will come across.

Exercise
Use the correct Demonstratives for these situations

1) "that" referring to something that is far from the speaker but close to the listener.

2) this tv
(tv = terebi テレビ)

3) here

4) "there" referring to something that is far from the listener and speaker

5) "that way" referring to something that is far from the listener but close to the speaker

Answers
1) sore それ
2) kono terebi このテレビ
3) koko ここ
4) asoko あそこ
5) sochira そちら

Super Simple Structure
とても基本的な文章構造

Now that we have a basic understanding of Japanese, let's go through a very useful sentence structure.

A wa B desu
(A is B)

This expression can be used in a variety of situations, making it extremely useful for beginners. A is always a noun, while B can be a noun or an adjective.

Desu and its uses
Desu is known as "verb to be" and refers to "is" "am" "are".

Example sentence:
Watashi wa John desu
私はジョンです
(Watashi 私= I)
I am John

If we were going to translate this literally it would be:

(as for me, John am)

However when we translate this, it becomes "I am john"

Once thing to remember, desu is a polite copula and is only used in formal speech. For informal speech we would omit "desu".

Now let's look at some examples using A is B structure.

She is a university student
Kanojo wa daigakusei desu
彼女は大学生です
(Kanojo 彼女 = she) (Daigakusei 大学生 = university student)
As for her, university student is.

A = she
B = univeristy student

The library is quiet
Toshokan wa shizuka desu
図書館は静かです
(Toshokan 図書館= library) (Shizuka 静か= quiet)
As for the library, quiet is

A = library
B = quiet

The coffee is tasty

Koohii wa oishi desu
コーヒーはおいしいです
(Koohii コーヒー = coffee) (Oishii おいしい = tasty)
As for coffee, tasty is.

A = coffee
B = oishi

We can use this structure with the previous demonstratives we have learnt to form more sentences.

This is cold

Kore wa samui desu
これは寒いです
(this = kore これ) (cold = samui 寒い)

That house is big

Ano ie wa ōkī desu
あの家は大きいです
(house = ie 家) (big = oki 大きい)

The structure A is B desu, can also be used when saying (A am B) or (A are B).

Examples
I am a teacher
Watashi wa sensei desu
私は先生です
(I = watashi 私) (teacher = sensei 先生)
As for me, teacher am

*Note
In Japanese there is no indefinite article "a/an" so we just omit this.

They are fast
Karera wa hayai desu
彼らは速いです
(fast = hayai 速い)

Like previously stated we can omit the subject if it is clear who we are talking about:

Examples
I am john
Watashi wa John desu
私はジョンです

I am a student

~~Watashi wa~~ gakusei desu
私は学生です
= gakusei desu 学生です

This way is Jaden
Kochira wa Jaden desu
こちらはジェーデンです

He is a doctor.
~~Kare wa~~ isha desu
~~彼は~~医者です
= isha desu 医者です

If it is confusing and we want to clarify, then we can add the subject.

Exercise:
Translate these sentences:

1. I am American
(American = amerikajin アメリカ人)(I = watashi 私)

Answer:
Watashi wa amerikajin desu
私はアメリカ人です

2. This is a library

(library = toshokan 図書館)

Answer:
Sore wa toshokan desu
それは図書館です

3. Mr. Sato is a teacher
(Sato san 佐藤さん = Mr. Sato) (Sensei 先生= teacher)

Answer:
Sato san wa sensei desu
佐藤さんは先生です

4. I am an office worker
(Kaishain 会社員 = office worker)

Answer:
Watashi wa kaishain desu
私は会社員です

**Hey! Hopefully Japanese is beginning to click for you. Pop by amazon and give us a quick review to say what you think of the book so far.

Desu Conjugation です活用形

Conjugation is when we change a verb/adjective to create a new meaning. In this section we will be conjugating the verb "desu です" to form even more sentences.

When we conjugate desu, we can make statements like:

Positive Present = A is B

Negative Present = A is not B

Positive Past = A was B

Negative Past = A was not B

Let's look at the four types of conjugation for desu

1. Positive Present = desu です
2. Negative Present
= ja nai desu じゃないです
= ja arimasen じゃありません
3. Positive Past = deshita でした
4. Negative Past
= ja nakatta desu じゃなかったです
= ja arimasen deshita じゃありませんでした

Let's look at examples of "desu" conjugation, to make better sense of them.

Example
1. I am a student
= watashi wa gakusei desu 私は学生です

2. I am not a student
= watashi wa gakusei ja nai
私は学生じゃない (inf)
= watashi wa ja arimasen
私はじゃありません (f)

3. I was a student
= watashi wa gakusei deshita 私は学生でした

4. I was not a student
= watashi wa gakusei ja nakatta
私は学生じゃなかった (inf)
= watashi wa gakusei ja arimasen deshita
私は学生じゃありませんでした (f)

We will go into all of these conjugations in detail below. We have already covered desu so let's begin with the present negative:

Present Negative (A is not B):

We use "ja nai じゃない" and "ja arimasen じゃありません" to make negative present tense sentences. For a more casual tone, we add **janai** じゃない before **desu** です and for a more formal tone we use **ja arimasen** じゃありません.

A is not B:

A wa B desu →   **A wa B** ja nai
or
A wa B desu →   **A wa B** ja arimasen

Examples:
Sensei desu
先生です
= I am a teacher

Sensei ja arimasen (f)
先生じゃありません
= I am not a teacher

Isha desu
医者です
= I am a doctor

Isha ja arimasen (f)
医者じゃありません
= I am not a doctor

(doctor = isha 医者)

Bengoshi desu
弁護士です
= I am a laywer

Bengoshi ja arimasen (f)
弁護士じゃありません
(laywer = bengoshi 弁護士)
= I am not a laywer

Kanojo wa daigakusei ja nai (inf)
彼女は大学生じゃない
(Kanojo 彼女 = she)
(Daigakusei 大学生 = university student)
She is not a university student

Senkou wa nihongo ja arimasen (f)
専攻は日本語じゃありません
(Senkou 専攻 = major)
(Nihongo 日本語 = Japanese)
My major is not Japanese language

Past Positive (A was B):
Now let's look at using **desu** in the past positive tense.

A was B

A wa B desu →   A wa B deshita (A was B)

Example sentences:

Senkou wa bijinesu deshita
専攻はビジネスでした
(Senkou 専攻 = major)
(Bijinesu ビジネス = business)
My major was business

Tanaka san wa isha deshita
田中さんは医者でした
(Tanaka san = Mr. Tanaka) (Isha 医者 = doctor)
Tanaka san was a doctor

Past Negative (A was not B):
When expressing 'A was not B', we use **ja nakatta desu** じゃなかったです for a more casual tone, and formally we use **ja arimasen deshita** じゃありませんでした.

A was not B

A wa B janai →   A wa B ja nakatta (inf)
A wa B ja arimasen + deshita   →   A wa B ja arimasen deshita (f)

Example sentences:

Senkou wa bijinesu ja nakatta (inf)
専攻はビジネスじゃなかった
(Senkou 専攻 = major)
(Bijinesu ビジネス = business)
My major was not business

Tanaka san wa isha ja arimasen deshita (f)
田中さんは医者じゃありませんでした
(Tanaka san = Mr. Tanaka) (Isha 医者 = doctor)
Tanaka san was a not doctor

Exercise:
Translate the sentences into Japanese.

1. The girl is 8 years old
(Girl = onna no ko 女の子)
(8 years old = hassai 八才)

Answer:
Onna no ko wa hassai desu.
女の子は八才です

2. The boy is not an elementary school student
(Casual)
(Boy = otoko no ko 男の子) (Elementary school student = shougakusei 小学生)

Answer:
Otoko no ko wa shougakusei janai

男の子は小学生じゃない

3. He was a politician
(He = kare) (Politician = seijika)

Answer:
Kare wa seijika deshita.
彼は政治家でした

4. Kim was not an actress (Formal)
(Friend = tomodachi 友達)
(Actress = joyuu 女優)

Answer:
Kim wa joyuu ja arimasen deshita.
キムは女優じゃありませんでした

Possessive Pronouns 所有代名詞

Possessive pronouns refer to words like "my" "your" "his" etc. In Japanese we have to use the particle "no の" to make these words. The particle "no の" is used to show possession.

Here is a list of possessive pronouns

My	=	Watashi no 私の
Yours	=	Anata no あなたの
Your (plural)	=	Anata tachi no あなた達の
His	=	Kare no 彼の
Hers	=	Kanojo no 彼女の
Ours	=	Watashi tachi no 私達の
Theirs	=	Karera no 彼らの
Its	=	Sore no, Kore no, Are no それの、これの、あれの

As we have seen in the "Introduction" we use the particle 'no の' to say 'my name':

"My name"
Watashi no namae
私の名前"

By simply adding a noun after the possessive pronoun with the particle "no", we can make a possessive sentence.

Language pattern

Pronoun   +   "no"   +   Noun

Examples
My teacher
= Watashi no Sensei
私の先生
(Teacher = Sensei 先生)

His girlfriend
= Kare no Kanojo
彼の彼女
(Girlfriend = Kanojo 彼女)

Your notebook
= Anata no nooto
あなたのノート
(Notebook = Nooto ノート)

Their school
= Karera no gakko
彼の学校
(School = Gakko 学校)

Remember as stated before, in Japanese we avoid using, "you / your". Instead when we want to say 'you' or 'your' we use the name of the person instead.

Example:
~~Your~~ notebook
= ~~Anata~~ no nooto
~~あなた~~のノート
John's notebook
= John san no nooto
ジョンさんのノート
(Notebook = Nooto ノート)

~~His~~ friend
= ~~Kare~~ no tomodachi
彼の友達
Yoshida's friend
= Yoshida san no tomodachi
吉田さんの友達
(Friend = tomodachi 友達)

Whenusing the particle "no の", it also refers to the **'s** in English.
Therefore when we say things like sam's shoe**'s** or the man**'s** hat, we have to use "no の":

Examples
The dog's leg
Inu no ashi
犬の足
(dog = inu 犬) (leg = ashi 足)

Canadian winter
Translates to Canada's winter
Kanada no fuyu
カナダの冬
(winter = fuyu 冬)

Suzuki's bag
Suzuki no kaban
鈴木のカバン
(bag = kaban カバン)

Let's see some examples of "no" in sentences

This is his book
Kore wa kare no hon desu
これは彼の本です
(book = hon 本)

That is not my car
Sore wa watashi no kuruma ja arimasen
それは私の車じゃありません
(car = kuruma 車)

That is Yumi's dog
Sore wa Yumi san no inu desu
それは由美さんの犬です
(dog = inu 犬)

Exercise
Translate the following phrase

1) His dog
(dog = inu 犬)

2) Jake's bike
(bike = jitensha 自転車)

3) The cat's food
(food = tabemono 食べ物) (cat = neko 猫)

4) My car
(car = kuruma 車)

Answers
1) Kare no inu 彼の犬
2) Jake no jitensha ジェイクの自転車
3) Neko no tabemono 猫の食べ物
4) Watashi no kuruma 私の車

Like / Dislike 好き/好きじゃない

To state things that we like or dislike in Japanese, we use two phrases:

These are "suki na 好きな" (to like) and "kirai na 嫌いな" (to hate).

These are both "na" adjectives, we will go through "na" adjectives in a later section, but first let's get familiar with this language pattern:

Sentence structure:

   X wa Y ga Suki desu   =   **X likes Y.**

   X wa **Y** ga Kirai desu   =   **X hates Y.**

In this structure we have a new particle "ga が". Ga can be confusing to understand until you know more Japanese. So we will leave this out until we reach the particle section. In this section we really want you to focus on this language pattern instead.

Let's see some examples in use:

I like fish.
Watashi wa Sakana ga suki desu
私は魚が好きです
(sakana 魚 = fish)

Yuko hates mathematics.
Yuko san wa sugaku ga kirai desu
ゆこさんは数学が嫌いです
(suuaku 数学 = mathematics)

Like with other parts of Japanese we can omit the subject if it is clear:

I like Japan
~~Watashi wa~~ Nihon ga suki desu
~~私は~~日本が好きです
= Nihon ga suki desu
日本が好きです
(Japan = Nihon 日本)

When stating things that you don't like, it is better to use the negative form of suki (suki ja arimasen/ja nai). This is because the word "kirai 嫌い" is very strong and expresses an extreme dislike/hate.

I don't like sushi
(Watashi wa) sushi ga suki ja arimasen
(私は）寿司が好きじゃありません

I don't like cats (inf)
(Watashi wa) neko ga suki ja nai
(私は）猫は好きじゃない

Now if you are neutral, and neither like or dislike something, you can use this phrase:

X wa Y ga suki demo kirai demo arimasen
(neither like or dislike)

Example:
I neither like nor dislike fish
Watashi wa sakana ga suki demo kirai demo arimasen
私は魚が好きでも嫌いでもありません
(Sakana 魚 = fish)

I neither like nor dislike school
Watashi wa gakko ga suki demo kirai demo arimasen
私は学校が好きでも嫌いでもありません
(gakko 学校 = school)

Exercise
Now it's your turn, translate these phrases

1) I like Japanese food

(Japanese food = nipponshoku 日本食)

2) I don't like Monday
(Monday = getsuyobi 月曜日)

3) I neither like or dislike cake
(cake = keki ケーキ)

Answers
1) Watshi wa nipponshoku ga suki desu
私は日本食が好きです

2) Watashi wa getsuyobi ga suki ja arimasen
私は月曜日が好きじゃありません

3) Watashi wa keki ga suki demo kirai demo arimasen
私はケーキが好きでも嫌いでもありません

Question Marker "ka"
クエスチョンマーク"か"

"ka" is a question marking particle and used to make questions in Japanese. To make a sentence into a question, we add "ka" to the end.

Sentence structure

Sentence   +   ka?

Examples:
Sentence 1

Anata wa Sushi ga suki desu
あなたは寿司が好きです
= You like Sushi

Anata wa Sushi ga suki desu ka?
あなたは寿司が好きですか
= Do you like Sushi?

Sentence 2

Tokyo wa kirei desu
東京は綺麗です
= Tokyo is clean.

Tokyo wa kirei desu ka?

東京は綺麗ですか
= Is Tokyo clean?
(Kirei 綺麗 = clean)

Sentence 3
Kore wa anata no inu desu
これはあなたの犬です
= **This is your dog**
(dog = inu 犬)

Kore wa anata no inu desu ka?
これはあなたの犬ですか
= **Is this your dog?**

We can answer these question, with the same A is B pattern. Let's look at some questions and answers together:

Anata wa Sushi ga suki desu ka?
あなたは寿司が好きですか
= Do you like Sushi?

Hai, (watashi wa) sushi ga suki desu
はい、（私は）寿司が好きです
= Yes, I like Sushi.
(yes = hai はい)

Iie, (watashi wa) sushi ga suki ja arimasen
(いいえ、私は）寿司が好きじゃありません
= No, I don't like sushi.

(no = iie いいえ)

Tokyo wa kirei desu ka?
東京は綺麗ですか？
= **Is Tokyo clean?**
(clean = kirei 綺麗)

Hai, Tokyo wa kirei desu
はい、東京は綺麗です
= **Yes, Tokyo is clean.**

Iie, Tokyo wa kirei ja arimasen
いいえ、東京は綺麗じゃありません
= **No, Tokyo isn't clean.**

We can even simply say yes or no:
Kore wa anata no inu desu ka?
これはあなたの犬ですか
= **Is this your dog?**

Hai はい
= **Yes**

Iie いいえ
= **No**

For informal speech we don't use "ka", instead we use a rising tone to ask questions:

Tokyo wa kirei?
東京は綺麗 (inf)
= **Is Tokyo clean?**

Kore wa anata no inu?
これはあなたの犬
= **Is this your dog?**

Remember in informal speech we omit desu. There is another way to make questions in informal speech, this is by adding the particle "no の" at the end.

Exercises:
Change these statements into sentences

1) This food is hot
Kono tabemono atsui desu
この食べ物熱いです
(food = tabemono 食べ物)

2) Yuri is his younger sister (casual)
Kare no imoto wa Yuri
彼の妹はゆり
(younger sister = imoto 妹)

3) This phone is expensive

Kono denwa takai desu
この電話高いです
(phone = denwa 電話) (expensive = takai 高い)

Answers
1) Is this food is hot?
Kono tabemono atsui desu ka?
この食べ物熱いですか

2) Is Yuri is his younger sister? (casual)
Kare no imoto wa Yuri
彼の妹はゆり (rising tone)

3) Is this phone is expensive?
Kono denwa takai desu ka?
この電話は高いですか

Question Word: Whose? 疑問形:誰の

Let's go through the question word "whose" which is "dare no 誰の".

One thing to keep in mind, when using question words you also need to use the question particle "ka か" at the end of the sentence.

Whose　　　　　　=　　Dare no 誰の

Example

Whose Umbrella is this? = Dare no kasa desu ka? 誰の傘ですか

It is my umbrella = Watashi no kasa desu 私の傘です
(Umbrella = kasa 傘)

This question word is often used in combination with "kore これ, sore それ, are あれ" words

Whose book is this?
= Kore wa dare no hon desu ka?
これは誰の本ですか

That is my book

= Sore wa watashi no hon desu
それは私の本です
(Book = Hon 本)

Whose bag is that?

= Are wa dare no kaban desu ka?
あれは誰のカバンですか

That is Honda's bag

= Are wa Honda san no kaban desu
あれは本田さんのカバンです
(Bag = Kaban カバン)

Adjectives 形容詞

Moving onto adjectives, in Japanese we have two types of adjectives.

They are called, "i adjectives" and "na adjectives".

<u>i adjectives:</u> end with "i" sound
Examples:

       Kawaii かわいい   **cute**
       Wakai 若い   **young**
       Ookii 大きい   **big**
       Chiisai 小さい   **small**
       Omoshiroi 面白い   **interesting**
       Isogashii 忙しい   **busy**
       Kowaii 怖い   **scary**
       Oishii おいしい   **tasty/delicious**

<u>Na- adjectives:</u> end with "na" sound
Examples:

       Kirei na 綺麗な   **clean**
       Shizuka na 静かな   **quiet**
       Genki na 元気な   **cheerful**
       Taikutsu na 退屈な   **boring**

Hima na 暇な　　　　　　free time
Nigiyaka na にぎやかな　lively

We can use these adjectives in the same basic sturucture pattern, A is B

Yoko is cute
Yoko san wa kawaii desu
洋子さんはかわいいです

Winter in Canada is cold
Kanada no fuyu wa samui desu
カナダの冬は寒いです

(remember no particle is needed because you are referring to Canada's winter)

When using these adjectives, we use them in different ways

'I adjectives' remain the same and do not change:

Examples
She is young
= (Kanojo wa) wakai desu
= (彼女は）若いです
(young = wakai 若い)

I am busy
= (Watashi wa) isogashī desu
= (私は) 忙しいです
(busy = isogashi 忙しい)

With "Na- adjective", when the pattern is "Subject is adjective", the last "na" is dropped.

Kirei na 綺麗な
(beautiful/clean)

1. Drop "Na" Kirei ~~na~~   →   Kirei
2. Add "desu"   Kirei   →   Kirei + desu

Example
Subject is adjective
Yumi is beautiful
Yumi san wa kirei desu.
由美さんは綺麗です

I am free
(Watashi wa) hima desu.
(私は) 暇です

Another way to think of it:
"na" depends on the position of the adjective:

If the na adjective is before the noun, we add "na".

If the na adjective is after the noun we remove "na".

Adjective before the noun:
Yūmei**na** gakkō desu.
有名な学校です
It is a famous school.

Adjective after the noun:
Kono gakkō wa yūmei desu.
この学校は有名です
This school is famous.

So when it comes to adjectives, it's good practice to remembering what type each adjective is, aswell as its meaning.

Even though some na adjectives maybe tricky to determine. You can always find out the type of an adjective by the sound they end in.

Exercise
Translate these sentences into Japanese

1) This textbook is interesting.
(textbook = kyokasyo 教科書)

2) It is my pretty sister.
(sister = imoto 妹)

3) I like this quiet café.
(café = kafe カフェ)

Answers

1) This textbook is interesting.
Kono kyoukasyo wa omosiroi desu.
この教科書は面白いです

2) It is my pretty sister.
Kore wa watashi no kawaii imoto desu.
これは私のかわいい妹です

3) I like this quiet café.
Watashi wa kono shizuka na kafe ga suki desu.
私はこの静かなカフェが好きです

I Adjective Conjugation
い形容詞活用形

Now that we know the basics of *i* – adjectives, we going to learn how to conjugate them to make more forms and tenses.

Let's look at the conjugations with the example i-adjective "kawaii かわいい":

There are four types of conjugation for 'i' adjectives
1. Positive Present = kawaii かわいい
2. Negative Present
= kawaikunai かわいくない
= kawaiku arimasen かわいくありません
3. Positive Past = kawaikatta かわいかった
4. Negative Past
= kawaikunakatta
= kawaiku arimasen deshita かわいくありませんでした

Example
1. I am cute = watashi wa kawaii desu 私はかわいいです
2. I am not cute
= watashi wa kawaikunai desu 私はかわいくないです

= kawaiku arimasen かわいくありません

3. I was cute = watashi wa kawaikatta 私はかわいかった

4. I was not cute

= watashi wa kawaikunakatta 私はかわいくなかった

= kawaiku arimasen deshita かわいくありませんでした

Negative Present (not cute):

To make negative present, you simply remove the last 'i' from the adjective and replace it with **kunai** くない or a more formal **ku arimasen** くありません.

Kawaii (cute) → kawai + kunai → kawaikunai **(not cute)**

Kawaii (cute) → kawai + ku arimasen → kawaiku arimasen **(not cute)**

Examples:
Ookii 大きい(big)
→　　ookikunai 大きくない(not big)

Chiisai 小さい(small)
→	chiisaku arimasen 小さくありません (not small)

Isogashii 忙しい (busy)
→	isogashikunai 忙しくない (not busy)

Omoshiroi 面白い(interesting)
→	omoshiroku arimasen 面白くありません (not interesting)

There are some adjectives that are irregular that dont follow this pattern. But luckily it's only two:

! (Irregular adjective)
Ii いい (good)
→	yokunai よくない (not good)

! (Irregular adjective)
Kakkoii かっこいい (handsome)
→	kakkoyoku arimasen かっこよくありません(not handsome)

Positive Past (was cute):

To make positive past tense 'i' adjectives, the last 'i' of the adjective is removed and replaced by **katta かった**.

Kawaii (cute) → kawai + katta → kawaikatta **(was cute)**

Examples:
Ookii 大きい (big)
→ ookikatta 大きかった (was big)

Chiisai 小さい (small)
→ chiisakatta 小さかった (was small)

Isogashii 忙しい (busy)
→ isogashikatta 忙しかった (was busy)

Omoshiroi 面白い (interesting)
→ omoshirokatta 面白かった (was interesting)

! (Irregular adjective)
Ii いい (good)
→ yokatta よかった (was good)

! (Irregular adjective)
Kakkoii かっこいい (handsome)
→ kakkoyokatta かっこよかった (was handsome)

Negative Past (was not cute):

To make a negative past tense adjective, the last 'i' of the negative form adjective is removed and replaced by **kunakatta** くなかった, or using a more formal tone is **ku arimasen deshita** くありませんでした.

Kawaikunai → kawaikunakatta *(was not cute)*
Kawaikuarimasen + deshita →kawaiku arimasen deshita *(was not cute)*

Examples:
Ookikunai 大きくない (not big)
→ ookikunakatta 大きくなかった (was not big)

Chiisakuarimasen 小さくありません (not small)

→ chiisaku arimasen deshita 小さくありませんでした (was not small)

Isogashikunai 忙しくない (not busy)
→ isogashikunakatta 忙しくなかった (was not busy)

Omoshirokuarimasen 面白くありません (not interesting)
→ omoshiroku arimasen deshita 面白くありませんでした (was not interesting)

! (Irregular adjective)
Yokunai よくない (not good)
→   yokunakatta よくなかった (was not good)

! (Irregular adjective)
Kakkoyoku arimasen かっこよくありません (not handsome)
→   Kakkoyoku arimasen deshita かっこよくありませんでした (was not handsome)

Exercise:
Translate the sentences into Japanese.
1. The car is expensive.
(Car = kuruma 車) (Expensive = takai 高い)

Answer:
Kuruma wa takai desu.
車は高いです

2. The movie is not scary.
(Movie = eiga 映画) (Scary = kowai 怖い)

Answer:
Eiga wa kowaikunai desu.
映画は怖いです

3. The newspaper was interesting.
(Newspaper = shinbun 新聞) (Interesting = omoshiroi 面白い)

Answer:
Shinbun wa omoshirokatta desu.
新聞は面白かったです

4. The dinner was not tasty.
(Dinner = bangohan 晩御飯) (Tasty = Oishii おいしい)

Answer:
Bangohan wa oishikunakatta desu.
晩御飯はおいしいです

5. The house was not big. (Polite)
(House = ie 家) (Big = Ookii 大きい)

Answer:
Ie wa ookikuarimasen deshita.
家は大きくありませんでした

Na Adjective Conjugation
な形容詞活用形

Luckily you don't have to remember another conjugation because na – adjective conjugation is the same as **desu** conjugation.

There are four types of conjugation for na adjectives
1. Positive Present = (na な)
2. Negative Present
 = ja nai desu じゃないです
 = ja arimasen じゃありません
3. Positive Past = deshita でした
4. Negative Past
= ja nakatta desu じゃなかったです
= ja arimasen deshita じゃありませんでした

Example
1. I am beautiful = watashi wa kirei (na) desu 私は綺麗（な）です
2. I am not beautiful
= watashi wa kirei ja nai (desu)私は綺麗じゃない（です）
= /ja arimasen じゃありません
3. I was beautiful = watashi wa kirei deshita 私は綺麗でした
4. I was not beautiful

= watashi wa kirei ja nakatta desu 私は綺麗じゃなかったです
= /ja arimasen deshita じゃありませんでした

Negative Present (not beautiful):
Kirei ~~na~~ (beautiful)　Kirei desu
　　　kirei janai desu (inf)
Kirei ~~na~~ (beautiful)　Kirei ~~desu~~
　　　kirei ja arimasen (f)

Examples:
Shizuka na (quiet) 静かな
shizuka janai desu (not quiet) 静かじゃないです

Genki na (cheerful) 元気な
genki ja arimasen (not cheerful) 元気じゃありません

Taikutsu na (boring) 退屈な
taikutsu janai desu (not boring) 退屈じゃないです

Hima na (free, spare time) 暇な
hima ja arimasen (not free) 暇じゃありません

Nigiyaka na (lively) にぎやかな
nigiyaka janai desu (not lively) にぎやかじゃないです

Yuumei na (famous) 有名な
yuumei ja arimasen (not famous) 有名じゃありません

Positive Past (was beautiful):
Kirei na (beautiful)　　　Kirei desu　　kirei deshita

Examples:
Shizuka na (quiet) 静かな
shizuka deshita (was quiet) 静かでした

Genki na (cheerful) 元気な
genki deshita (was cheerful) 元気でした

Taikutsu na (boring) 退屈な
taikutsu deshita (was boring) 退屈でした

Hima na (spare time) 暇な
hima deshita (was free) 暇でした

Nigiyaka na (lively) にぎやかな
nigiyaka deshita (was lively) にぎやかでした

Yuumei na (famous) 有名な
yuumei deshita (was famous) 有名でした

Negative Past (was not beautiful):

Kirei janai (not beautiful)   →   kirei ja nakatta desu (inf)

Kirei ja arimasen (not beautiful)   Kirei ja arimasen + deshita   →Kirei ja arimasen deshita (f)

Examples:

Shizuka janai desu (not quiet)
静かじゃないです

shizuka ja nakatta desu (was not quiet)
静かじゃなかったです

Genki ja arimasen (not cheerful)
元気じゃありません

genki ja arimasen deshita (was not cheerful)
元気じゃありませんでした

Taikutsu janai desu (not boring) 退屈じゃないです

taikutsu ja nakatta desu (was not boring)
退屈じゃなかったです

Hima ja arimasen (not free)
暇じゃありません

hima ja arimasen deshita (was not free)
暇じゃありませんでした

Nigiyaka janai desu (not lively)
にぎやかじゃないです

nigiyaka ja nakatta desu (was not lively)
にぎやかじゃなかったです

Yuumei ja arimasen (not famous)
有名じゃありません

yuumei ja arimasen deshita (was not famous)
有名じゃありませんでした

Exercise:
Translate the given sentences:

1. The town is quiet
(town = machi 町) (quiet = shizuka na 静かな)

Answer:
Machi wa shizuka desu.
町は静かです

2. My friend is not cheerful (Casual)
(friend = tomodachi 友達)
(cheerful = genki na 元気な)

Answer:
Tomodachi wa genki janai desu.
友達は元気じゃないです

3. The move was boring
(movie = eiga 映画)
(boring = taikutsu na 退屈な)

Answer:

Eiga wa taikutsu deshita.
映画は退屈でした

4. The actress was not famous

(Actress = joyuu 女優)

(Famous = yumei na 有名な)

Answer:

Joyuu wa yumei ja arimasen deshita.
女優は有名じゃありませんでした

Number in Japanese 日本語の数字

Japanese number system is very easy to learn. Once you can count from 1 to 10, you can combine these numbers to count up to 99. Some numbers have two forms and using them depends on the function of the number e.g. time (hour and minute), counter word, etc...

Below is a list of the first 10 numbers:

1 Ichi 一
2 Ni 二
3 San 三
4 Yon/shi 四
5 Go 五
6 Roku 六
7 Nana/Shichi 七
8 Hachi 八
9 Kyu/ku 九
10 Juu 十

When you want to make numbers larger than 10, we combine the separate parts of these numbers together:

e.g. 11
10 + 1 Juu + ichi → Juu ichi 十一

e.g. 34
3 + 10 + 4   San + Juu + Yon   →   San ju yon 三十四

There are two ways to say numbers 4, 7 and 9. However, when you make 40, 70, and 90, the following phrases are always applied:

40 = Yon juu 四十   **70 =** Nana juu 七十
90 = Kyuu juu 九十

Bigger numbers are as follows:

100 = Hyaku 百
1,000 = Sen 千
10,000 = Man 万

There are some exceptions.
The following numbers have different pronunciation:

300   **San** Byak 三百
3,000   **San** Zen 三千
600   Roppyaku 六百
800   Happyaku 八百

In Japanese it is a good idea to get familiar with larger number because Japanese currency get big very quickly.

Exercise:

Translate the list of number below.

18   = ...
35   = ...
97   = ...
138 = ...
824 = ...
200 = ...
5000 = ...
1630 = ...

Answer:

18
Jyuu + hachi
= Jyuuhachi
十八

35
San + jyuu + go
= Sanjyuugo
三十五

97
Kyuu + jyuu + nana

= Kyuujyuunana
九十七

138
Hyaku + san + jyuu+ hachi
= Hyakusanjyuuhachi
百三十八

824
Hachi + hyaku + ni + jyuu + yon
= Happyaku nijyuuyon
八百二十四

200
Ni + hyaku
= Ni hyaku
二百

5000
Go + sen
= Go sen
五千

1630
Sen + roku + hyaku + san + jyuu
= Senroppyaku sanjyuu
千六百三十

Question Word: How Much?
質問形:どれくらい

Now that we have a better understanding of numbers, we can learn how to ask for price in Japanese:

To ask for the price of an item we use the following phrase:

How much is it? = Ikura desu ka? **(f)** いくらですか

                     = **Ikura (inf)** いくら

It's …. yen. = …. en desu **(f)** 円です
                     = … en **(inf)** 円

Japanese currency is "yen" and is pronounced as "en".

Examples:

300 yen	=	San byaku en 三百円
7600 yen	=	Nana sen roppyaku en 七千六百円
15000 yen	=	Ichi man go sen en

一万五千円

823 yen = Happyaku nijuu san en
八百二十三円

We can also combine this with the ko-so-do-a words to be more specific about items:

Examples:
Sore wa ikura desu ka?
それはいくらですか
= How much is that?

Kono hon wa ikura desu ka?
この本はいくらですか
= How much is this book?
(Book = hon 本)

Ano kaban wa ikura desu ka?
あのかばんはいくらですか
= How much is that bag?
(Bag = Kaban カバン)

Remember, kono/sono/ano is used when talk about a specific noun.

Exercise
Translate the given sentences:

1. How much is this ticket? It's 3,000 yen.
(ticket = chiketto チケット)

Answer:
Kono chiketto wa ikura desu ka? Sanzen en desu.
このチケットはいくらですか？三千円です

2. How much is that bouquet? It's 1200 yen.
(bouquet = hanataba 花束)

Answer:
Ano hanataba wa ikura desu ka? Sen nihyaku en desu.
あの花束はいくらですか？千二百円です

3. How much is the rice? It's 1800 yen.
(rice = okome お米)

Answer:
Sono okome wa ikura desu ka? Sen happyaku en desu.
そのお米はいくらですか？千八百円です。

Japanese Verbs 日本語の動詞

Like adjectives, there are two types of verbs in Japanese. These are "u-verbs" and "ru-verbs".

Ru verbs end in the letters "iru" or "eru"
U verb end in 'u'

There are some exception to this rule, as some verbs ending in "iru" and "eru" are u verbs. So try to remember these exceptions when you come across them, to avoid getting confused.

Ru-verbs

Taberu 食べる	=	to eat
Neru 寝る	=	to sleep
Miru 見る	=	to see, to watch
Okiru 起きる	=	to wake up

U-verbs

Nomu 飲む	=	to drink
Kaku 書く	=	to write
Iku 行く	=	to go
Hanasu 話す	=	to speak
Hashiru 走る	=	to run (exception)
Kiku 聞く	=	to listen, to hear

Japanese also consists of two irregular verbs, since these verbs are irregular they do not fall into the catergories above.

Irr verbs
Kuru 来る = to come
Suru する = to do

Using "suru する"
Adding "-suru" to a noun can transform it into a verb.
For example,

Benkyo (Study) + Suru (to do)
= to study

Sentaku (laundry) + Suru (to do)
= to do laundry

The word "suru" can also be added to the name of a sport to state that you play that sport:

Examples:
    Sakkaa suru サッカーする =
    to play soccer
    Yakyuu suru 野球する =
    to play baseball

Tenisu suru テニスする   =
to play tennis

All the verbs listed above are in their informal forms, we will cover formal forms in the next section.

Particle 'o/wo を(お)'

When using verbs we need to use the particle 'o', this particle is also written as 'wo' but always pronounced as 'o'. A lot of beginners get confused by this.

The 'o' particle is used after an object. Without using the 'o' particle, it can be difficult to determine the object in the sentence.

Lets see some example of how to use the 'o' particle:

I eat sushi

(Watashi wa) sushi o taberu
私は寿司を（お）食べる
(eat = taberu 食べる)

Here sushi is the object we are talking about, therefore we need to mark this with the particle 'o' right after the word.

I drink water

Watashi wa mizu o nomu
私は水を（お）飲む
(water = mizu 水) (drink = nomu 飲む)

I listen to music

(Watashi wa 私は) ongaku o hiku
音楽を（お）聴く
(music = ongaku 音楽) (listen = kiku 聴く)

Exercise

Translate the given sentences:

1. I do my homework.
(homework = syukudai 宿題)

Answer:
Watashi wa syukudai o suru.
私は宿題を（お）する

2. His girlfriend goes to university.
(university = daigaku 大学)

Answer:
Kare no kanojyo wa daigaku ni iku.
彼の彼女は大学に行く

3. My big brother works at that company.

(big brother = ani 兄) (work = hataraku 働く)
(company = kaisya 会社)

Answer:
Watashi no ani wa ano kaisya de hataraku.
私の兄はあの会社で働く

4. My frind eats wasabi.
(friend = tomodachi 友達)

Answer:
Watashi no tomodachi wa wasabi o taberu.
私の友達はわさびを（お）食べる

Masu Verb Conjugation
ます動詞活用形

In the previous topic we have learnt the basic verbs in informal speech. If we want to use verbs in formal speech we need to conjugate into "masu" form.

It's handy to know masu form as it can be used in many situations.

There are four types of conjugation for masu
1. Positive Present = masu ます
2. Negative Present = masen ません
3. Positive Past = mashita ました
4. Negative Past = masen deshita ませんでした

We conjugate slightly differently depending on the type of verb we are using:

Positive Present (masu)

Ru-verbs:
1. Drop the final "ru"
2. Add "masu"

      e.g. Taberu (to eat) →   Tabe + masu
      →   Tabemasu

U-verbs:
1. Drop the final "u"
2. Add "-imasu"
    e.g. Kaku (to write) → Kak + imasu
    → Kakimasu
       Yomu (to read) → Yom + imasu
    → Yomimasu

Irregular verbs:

Kuru
1. Drop the final "uru"
2. Add "-imasu"
    e.g. Kuru (to come) → K + imasu
    → Kimasu

Suru
1. Drop the final "uru"
2. Add "-himasu"
    e.g. Suru (to do) → S + himasu
    → Shimasu

<u>Examples</u>

I eat sushi

Sushi o tabemasu

寿司を（お）食べます

I solve the problem

(to solve = toku 解く) (problem = mondai 問題)
Mondai o tokimasu
問題を（お）解きます

I ride a bike
(ride = noru 乗る)
Jitensya ni norimasu
自転車に乗ります

I study Japanese
Nihonngo o benkyou shimasu
日本語の勉強します

Negative Present:
The **masu** ending is replaced with **masen.**
**Taberu (to eat)   tabemasu
      tabemasen**
(r*u*-verb)

Examples:
    Neru (to sleep)   nemasu
    nemasen
    (*ru*-verb)
    Yomu (to read)   yomimasu
    yomimasen
    (*u*-verb)

    Suru (to do)   shimasu

shimasen
(irregular verb)

Sentence examples

I do not wake up
Okimasen
起きません

I do not buy it
Sore o kaimasen
それを（お）買いません

I do not go there
(there = asoko あそこ)
Asoko ni ikimasen
あそこに行きません

I do not drink juice
(juice = jyuusu ジュース)
Jyuusu o nomimasen
ジュースを（お）飲みません

Positive Past:

The **masu** ending is replaced with **mashita.**

Taberu (to eat)　　**tabemasu**

tabemashita

(r*u*-verb)

Examples:

    Neru (to sleep)   nemasu
    nemashita
    (*ru*-verb)

    Yomu (to read)   yomimasu
    yomimashita

    (*u*-verb)
    Suru (to do)   shimasu
    shimashita
    (irregular verb)

<u>Sentence examples</u>

I ate dinner
Bangohan o tabemashita
晩御飯を（お）食べました

I saw the sky
(sky = sora 空)
Sono sora o mimashita
その空を（お）見ました

I played soccer
Sakkaa o shimashita
サッカーを（お）しました

I watched a movie
(to watch = miru 観る)

Eiga o mimashita
映画を（お）観ました

Negative Past:
The **masu** ending is replaced with **masen deshita.**
> **Taberu (to eat)**   **tabemasu**
> **tabemasen deshita**
> (r*u*-verb)

Examples:
> Neru (to sleep)   nemasu
> nemasen deshita
> (*ru*-verb)

> Yomu (to read)   yomimasu
> yomimasen deshita
> (*u*-verb)

> Suru (to do)   shimasu
> shimasen deshita
> (irregular verb)

Sentence examples
I did not write a letter
(letter = tegami 手紙)
Tegami o kakimasen deshita
手紙を（お）書きませんでした

I did not visit my friend
(visit = otozureru 訪れる)
Tomodachi o otozuremasen deshita
友達を訪れませんでした

I did not talk with my mother
(mother = haha 母)
Haha to hanashimasen deshita
母と話しませんでした

I did not read the newspaper
(newspaper = shinbun 新聞)
Shinnbunn o yomimasen deshita
新聞を（お）読みませんでした

Now let's see these in longer sentences:

1. I do not go to school.
(I = watashi 私) (To go = iku 行く)
(School = gakko 学校)
Watashi wa gakko ni ikimasen.
私は学校に行きません

2. I do not watch scary movies.
(I = watashi 私) (To watch = miru 観る)
(Scary = kowai 怖い) (Movie = eiga 映画)
Watashi wa kowai eiga wo mimasen.
私は怖い映画を（お）観ません

3. I did the laundry.
(I = watashi 私) (To do laundry = sentaku suru 洗濯する)
Watashi wa sentaku shimashita.
私は洗濯しました

4. I did not do my homework.
(I = watashi 私) (Homework = shukudai 宿題) (To do = suru する)
Watashi wa shukudai o shimasen deshita.
私は宿題を（お）しませんでした

5. I don't watch television
(tv = terebi テレビ) (watch = mimasu 見ます)
Watashi wa terebi o mimasen.
私はテレビを（お）見ません

6. I ate breakfast.
(breakfast = asagohan 朝御飯)
(eat = tabemasu 食べます)
Asagohan o tabemashita.
朝ごはんを（お）食べました

7. I don't eat breakfast.
(breakfast = asagohan 朝御飯) (eat = tabemasu 食べます)
Asagohan o tabemasen.
朝御飯を（お）食べません

If you are unsure of some of the particles used don't worry, they will become clear once we reach the particle section.

Exercise:
Write the following words in masu-form

Change to masu present positive:
Iku 行く (to go)
Nomu 飲む (to drink)
Taberu 食べる (to eat)

Change to masu present negative:
Tetsudau 手伝う (to help)
Okuru 送る (to send, u-verb)
Kau 買う (to buy)

Change to masu past positive:
Kariru 借りる (to borrow)
Tsukuru 作る (to make, u-verb)
Tsukau 使う (to use)

Change to masu past negative:
Naosu 直す (to fix/ to correct)
Oshieru 教える (to tell, to teach)

Answers:

Iku 行く	=	Ikimasu 行きます
Nomu 飲む	=	Nomimasu 飲みます
Taberu 食べる	=	Tabemasu 食べます
Tetsudau 手伝う	=	Tetsudaimasen 手伝いません
Okuru 送る	=	Okurimasen 送りません
Kau 買う	=	Kaimasen 買いません
Kariru 借りる	=	Karimashita 借りました
Tsukuru 作る	=	Tsukurimashita 作りました
Tsukau 使う	=	Tsukaimashita 使いました
Naosu 直す	=	Naoshimasen deshita 直しませんでした
Oshieru 教える	=	Oshiemasen deshita 教えませんでした

Informal Verb Conjugation
敬語でない動詞の活用形

We can conjugation verbs in informal tense to create to meanings to sentences. Conjugation into informal tense is also based on the type of verb used.

Let's go through each conjugation, starting with present negative

Present Negative
Ru verbs
Verbs ending in iru and eru, we change the last ru to nai

Example
Taberu 食べる = tabenai 食べない

U verbs
For u verbs we change the u to anai
Nomu 飲む = Nomanai 飲まない

If the u verb ends in a (vowel + u), we replace u with wanai.

Example
Au 会う = awanai 会わない

Irregular verbs

The two irregular verbs are conjugated in the following way:

Kuru 来る = konai 来ない
Suru する = shinai しない

Past Positive
Ru verbs

Verbs ending in iru and eru, we change the last ru to ta

Example
Taberu 食べる = tabeta 食べた

U verbs

U verbs are a little bit more complicated and change depending on the specific ending:

Ku く = ita いた
Gu ぐ = ida いだ
U tsu ru う つ る = tta った
Nu bu mu ぬ ぶ む = nda んだ
Su す = shita した

Past Negative

To make the past negative of informal speech we change nai (from negative speech) to nakatta:
Examples

Nomanai 飲まない
= nomanakatta 飲まなかった

Tabenai 食べない
= tabenakatta 食べなかった

Examples in sentences
I don't watch tv
Terebi o minai テレビを（お）見ない

I don't write letters
Tegami o kakanai 手紙を（お）書かない

Exercise:
Translate the given sentences in informal form:

1. I do not drink beer.
(beer = biiru ビール)

Answer:
Watashi wa biiru o nomanai.
私はビールを（お）飲まない

2. Her father did not come here.
(father = chichi 父) (here = koko ここ)

Answer:

Kanojyo no chichi wa koko ni konakatta.
彼女の父はここに来なかった

3. My big sister met my boyfriend.
(big sister = ane 姉) (to meet = au 会う)

Answer:
Watashi no ane wa watashino kareshi ni atta.
私の姉は私の彼氏に会った

4. She flew to London.
(to fly = tobu 飛ぶ) (London = rondon ロンドン)

Answer:
Kanojyo wa rondon ni tonda.
彼女はロンドンに飛んだ

Future Tense & Time Expression
未来形と時間表現

Japanese does not have the future tense word "will", like in English.
Instead the present form is used to state actions that hapeen in the present or in the future.

Examples:
I eat sushi
= sushi o tabemasu
寿司を（お）食べます
I will eat sushi
= sushi o tabemasu
寿司を（お）食べます

He sleeps = kare wa nemasu 彼は寝ます
He will sleep = kare wa nemasu 彼は寝ます

As you see it can get confusing to tell the difference in tenses, because both phrases are the same.

So to make it clear we use time expressions to emphasize that something will happen in the future.

Ashita watashi wa yomimasu

明日私は読みます
= I **will** read tomorrow.
(Tomorrow = Ashita 明日)

Now the sentence is clearly talking about something that will happen in the future.

There are two types of time expressions, with particle "ni" and without.

<u>'Ni に' particle</u>
The particle 'ni' has many uses and one of them is to express time.

For non specific we don't use 'ni'
For specific time we use 'ni' after the time phrase

<u>Time expressions without particle "ni"</u>

Yesterday	=	Kinou 昨日
Today	=	Kyou 今日
Tomorrow	=	Ashita 明日
Morning	=	Asa 朝
Daytime	=	Hiru 昼
Evening	=	Yuugata 夕方
Night	=	Yoru 夜

This morning	=	Kesa 今朝
This evening	=	Konban 今晩
This night	=	Konya 今夜
This week	=	Konshu 今週
This weekend	=	Konshuu matsu 今週末
This month	=	Kongetsu 今月
This year	=	Kotoshi 今年
Next week	=	Raishuu 来週
Next weekend	=	Raishuumatsu 来週末
Next month	=	Raigetsu 来月
Next year	=	Rainen 来年
Last week	=	Senshuu 先週
Last weekend	=	Senshumatsu 先週末
Last month	=	Sengetsu 先月
Last year	=	Kyonen 去年

These time expressions do not require the particle "ni" because they are not specific times.

<u>Time expression with particle "ni"</u>
The time expressions that require the particle "ni" are numerical time expressions such as "at 7:00 AM" and specific days.

Examples:

1. Specific time

I eat breakfast at 7:00 am.
= shichiji ni asagohan o tabemasu.
七時に朝御飯を（お）食べます
(breakfast = asagohan 朝御飯)

2. Specific Day

I will watch this movie on Saturday.
= Doyobi ni kono eiga o mimasu.
土曜日にこの映画を（お）観ます

I will go next Tuesday.
= Raishu no kayobi ni ikimasu.
来週の火曜日に行きます
(raishuu 来週 = next week)
Literally means "next week Tuesday I will go"

Here is the list of days of the week in Japanese, for reference:
Days of the week

Monday	=	Getsuyobi 月曜日
Tuesday	=	Kayobi 火曜日
Wednesday	=	Suiyobi 水曜日

Thursday	=	Mokuyobi 木曜日
Friday	=	Kinyobi 金曜日
Saturday	=	Doyobi 土曜日
Sunday	=	Nichiyobi 日曜日

Exercise

Translate the given sentences:

1. I will meet my boyfriend tomorrow.

Answer:

Watashi wa watashi no kareshi ni ashita au.
私は私の彼氏に明日会う

2. I will go to Japan next month.

Answer:

Watashi wa raigetu nihon ni iku.
私は来月日本に行く

3. I will go to countryside on Wednesday
(countryside = inaka 田舎)

Answer:

Watashi wa suiyoubi inaka ni iku.
私は水曜日に田舎に行く

4. She will watch a movie with her mother this evening.

Answer:

Kanojyo wa kanojyo no haha to konban eiga o miru.

彼女は彼女の母と今晩映画を（お）観る

Particles 助詞

Particles play an essential part in Japanese and are used to modify the meaning of words. Therefore it is important to understand particles, as the meaning of sentences can change based on the particle used.

One thing to remember is particles can have more than one function. So don't be alarmed if you see them used in different situations.

Let's cover most important particles first:

Wa は particle
As covered before wa は is a topic marking particle and used to mark the topic of a sentence.

Wa は particle function II
Wa は can also be used to mark contrast between two sentences. In this case we mark the contrasting sentences with "wa は" and use the word "demo でも" (but).

Examples
I eat fish but don't eat meat

Sakana wa tabemasu demo niku wa tabemasen
魚は食べます、でも肉は食べません

Normally we would say "sakana o tabemasu 魚を（お）食べます" to say "I eat fish", however since we are contrasting this sentence with "I don't eat meat", we need to use "wa は".
So when we use "wa は" here, we put a lot of contrast between the two sentences.

More examples
I like dogs but not cats
Inu wa suki desu demo neko wa kirai desu
犬は好きです、でも猫は嫌いです

Again, here we would use "ga が" however we need to use "wa は" as we are contrasting both sentences.

Ga が particle
Ga が is commonly used to add emphasis.

Examples
Kore wa pen desu
これはペンです
= this is a pen

If I want to emphasis this statement, you replace wa は with ga が:

Kore ga pen desu
これがペンです
= THIS is a pen

A situation you could use this is, if you are talking to a baby and they don't know what this item is. You can use ga to say that "THIS" item is a pen. Or if you are in an argument and you want to empahisis something, such as "MOVIE A" is better, here you would use "ga が".

Ga が particle function II
Ga が particle is also used in set statements such as about existence and desires. We will cover these later in the book, so keep an eye out for these.

Ni に particle
As stated previously "ni に" is used as a time marking particle for specific time expressions. Such as specific days or times with numbers.

Ni に particle function II
"ni に" is also used to show movement, therefore it is used with words like "iku 行く" and "kuru 来る"

Examples

I go to the cinema
Eigakan ni ikimasu
映画館に行きます

The cat come to my house everyday
Neko wa mainichi uchi ni kimasu
猫は毎日うちに来ます

Here the use of ni に is showing the direction of movement, in this case "to the cinema" or "to my house".

Since particle "ni に" has many usages, it can be seen more than once in a sentence.

On Monday I go to the library
Getsuyobi ni toshokan ni ikimasu
月曜日に図書館に行きます

In this sentence the first "ni に" marks the time and the other marks the direction of movement.

De で particle
De is used to express where an action is taking place. It can be thought of as the word "at" or "in".

Example
Ill see a movie in the cinema

Eigakan de 映画館で
= in the cinema
I see a movie
= Eiga o mimasu 映画を（お）観ます

I see a movie in the cinema
= Eigakan de eiga o mimasu
映画館で映画を（お）観ます

At the resturant
= Restaurant de レストランで
Eat dinner
= bangohan o taberu 晩御飯を（お）食べる

I eat dinner at the restaurant (inf)
= Restaurant de bangohan o taberu
レストランで晩御飯を（お）食べる

So when you are stating where an action is happening, use the "de" particle

De で particle function II
The second function of "de で" is to state "by using" or "means of"

Example
I draw a picture with a pen
With a pen = actually means by using a pen
Pen de ei o kakimasu

ペンで絵を（お）描きます

I go to work by bus.
Basu de shigoto ni ikimasu
バスで仕事に行きます
(by using bus ...)

I write my name by pen
Pen de namae o kakimasu
ペンで名前を（お）書きます
(by using pen ...)

To と particle
This particle is used to connect two or more nouns, it refers to the word "and". Such as "A and B and C"

Example
Handburger potatoe and coke please
Hanbaga to potatoe to coke o kudasi
ハンバーガーとポテトとコークを（お）くだ さい

I like cake and fish
Keki to sakana ga suki desu
ケーキと魚が好きです

To particle function II
To can also be used to say "with"

John saw a movie with yoko

John wa yoko to eigo o mimashita
ジョンは洋子と映画を（お）観ました

Tomorrow I go on a date with minami

Ashita, miniami san to detto o shimasu
明日、みなみさんとデートを（お）します

Mo も particle

This particle is used to mean also, when we use this particle it takes the postion of the previous particle wa わ, ga が, o お

Ken is also Canadian

Ken san mo kanada jin desu
ケンさんのカナダ人です

That is also mine

Sore mo watashi no desu
それも私のです

O お particle

O お shows a direct object, a thing that is directly involved or affected by the event.

In the following sentences, "I drink coffee", "I watch a movie", "coffee" and "a movie" are direct objects. The particle "o お" comes after the direct object.

I drink coffee.   **Coffee + o**

in Japanese: Koohii o nomimasu.
日本語:コーヒーお 飲みます
(koohii コーヒー= coffee)

I watch a movie   **Movie + o**

In Japanese: Eiga o mimasu.
日本語:映画を お 観ます
(eiga 映画= movie)

This particle can also be referred to as "wo を" but is always pronounced as 'o お'

Exercise
Translate the given sentences:

1. I study Japanese but do not study English
(English = Eigo 英語)

Answer:
Watashi wa nihongo wa benkyou shimasu, demo eigo wa benkyou shimasen.
私は日本語は勉強します、でも英語は勉強しません

2. He goes to university on Friday.

Answer:

Kare wa kinyoubi ni daigaku ni ikimasu.
彼は金曜日に大学に行きます

3. I ordered coffee and cake at the café.
(order = tanomu 頼む)

Answer:

Watashi wa kafe de koohii to keki o tanonda
私はカフェでコーヒーとケーキを（お）頼んだ

4. She wrote a letter with the pen.

Answer:

Kanojyo wa pen de tegami wo kaita.
彼女はペンで手紙を書いた

Wh- Questions 質問形

At the start of this book we covered closed questions and question word "whose 誰の". Now let's look into making complex questions:

What	=	Nani 何
When	=	Itsu いつ
Where	=	Doko どこ
Who	=	Dare だれ
Which	=	Dono どの
How	=	Do yatte どうやって

Examples:

A: What do you do on weekend?
= Shuumatsu nani o shimasu ka?
週末は何をしますか

In this example weekend is the topic therefore in comes before the question word. Particle "wa は" is also omitted as weekend is a unspecfic time expression. Unspecific time expressions don't use particles.

A: When will you go to the United States?
= Itsu Amerika ni ikimasuka?

いつアメリカに行きますか

B: I will go next month.
 = Raigetsu ikimasu.
来月行きます

A: Where do you often study?
=Doko de yoku benkyo shimasu ka?
どこでよく勉強しますか

B: I often study in the library.
= Yoku Toshokan de benkyo shimasu.
よく図書館で勉強します

A: Who cleans on Saturday?
= Doyobi ni dare ga soji shimasu ka?
土曜日に誰が掃除しますか

B: My older brother cleans.
= Ani ga soji shimasu.
兄が掃除します
 (Ani = older brother)

A: How will you come to the concert?
= Do yatte konsaato ni kimasu ka?
どうやってコンサートに来ますか

B: I will got by train
= Densha de ikimasu.
電車で行きます

Exercise

Translate the given sentences:

1. When will you come to my house? I will go on Sunday.

(house = ie 家)

Answer:
Itsu watashi no ie ni kimasuka? Nichiyoubi ni ikimasu.
いつ私の家に来ますか？日曜日に行きます

2. Where do you work? I work in Tokyo.

Answer:
Doko de hatarakimasuka? Tokyo de hatarakimasu.
どこで働きますか？東京で働きます

3. Who teaches you math? My mother teaches me math.

(math = sugaku 数学)

Answer:
Dare ga anata ni sugaku o oshiemasuka? Watashi no haha ga oshiemasu.
誰があなたに数学を（お）教えますか？私の母が教えます

4. How did you go back to your dorm? I came back by train.
(to go back = kaeru 帰る) (dorm = ryo 寮)

Answer:
Do yatte ryo ni kaerimashitaka? Densya de kaerimashita.
どうやって寮に帰りましたか？電車で帰りました

5. What will you do this weekend? I will go to gym.
(gym = jimu ジム)

Answer:
Konsyumatu wa nani o shimasuka?
今週末は何を（お）しますか？ジムに行きます

Japanese Sentence Structure
日本語の文章構造

So for we have covered a lot of the elements of Japanese. Now let's see where they are placed in a sentence.

Sentence structure:

Topic + Time + Location + Object + Verb

Remember each part of this structure will require a particle.
Let's look at an example:

e.g.
Watashi wa nichiyobi ni toshokan de eigo o benkyoshimasu.
私は日曜日に図書館で英語の勉強をします
I study English at the library on Sunday

Topic = Watashi 私(I)
Time = Nichiyobi 日曜日(Sunday)
Location = Toshokan 図書館 (library)
Object = Eigo 英語 (English)
Verb = benkyoshimasu 勉強します (study)

If a sentence does not contain any of the listed topics you can omit these.

e.g.
1. Watashi wa doyoubi ni tenisu o shimasu.
私は土曜日にテニスを（お）します
(Tenisu テニス = tennis),
(Saturday = doyoubi 土曜日)
= **I play tennis on Saturday.**

2. Watashi no chichi wa mainichi 10:00 ji ni ie ni kaeri masu.
私の父は毎日十時に家に帰ります
(Chichi 父 = father), (ie 家 = to home),
(kaerimasu 帰ります = to come back)
= **My father comes home at 10:00 PM every day.**

3. Yoshida san wa toshokan de shinbun o yomimasu.
吉田さんは図書館で新聞を読みます
(shinbun 新聞 = newspaper)
(yomimasu 読みます = to read)
= **Ms. Yoshida reads newspaper in the library.**

Exercise
Now it's your turn:

Arrange the selection of words to form the outlined sentence:

1. I study English at the library on Sunday = ?

Watashi 私   =   I
Nichiyobi 日曜日   =   Sunday
Toshokan 図書館   =   Library
Eigo 英語   =   English
Benkyoshimasu 勉強します   =   to study
Wa は, ni に, de で, o を（お）

Answer:
Watashi wa nichiyobi ni toshokan de eigo o benkyo shimasu.
私は日曜日に図書館で英語を勉強します

2. He eats breakfast at 7:00 am at the café.

Kare 彼 = He
Tabemasu 食べます = to eat
Asagohan 朝御飯   = breakfast
Nana ji 七時 = 7:00 am
Kissaten 喫茶店 = Café
Wa は, de で, ni に, o を

Answer:
Kare wa nana ji ni kissaten de asagohan o tabemasu.

彼は七時に喫茶店で朝御飯を食べます

3. I eat sushi at a restaurant at night.
Watashi 私　= I
Tabemasu 食べます = to eat
Sushi 寿司　= Sushi
Resutoran レストラン = Restaurant
Night 夜 = Yoru
Wa は, de で, o を（お）

Answer:
Watashi wa yoru resutoran de sushi o tabemasu.
私は夜レストランで寿司を食べます

4. I go to school
Watashi 私　= I
Gakko 学校　= School
Iku 行く = Go
Wa は, ni に

Answer
watashi wa gakko ni ikimasu
私は学校に行きます
or
gakko ni ikimasu
学校に行きます
Remember in Japanese certain topics can be omitted if not necessary

5. I studied English at the library on Sunday

Watashi 私 = I
Nichiyobi 日曜日 = Sunday
Toshokan 図書館 = Library
Eigo 英語 = English
Benkyoshimashita 勉強しました = to study
Ha は, ni に, de で, o を（お）

Answer:
Watashi wa nichiyoubi ni toshokan de eigo o benkyo shimashita.
私は日曜日に図書館で英語を（お）勉強しました

6. She ate breakfast at 8:00 am at home.

Kanojo 彼女 = She
Tabemashita 食べました = ate
Asagohan 朝御飯 = breakfast
Hachi ji 八時 = 8:00 am
Uchi うち = Home
Wa は, de で, ni に, o を（お）

Answer:
Kanojo wa hachi ji ni uchi de asagohan o tabemashita.
彼女は八時にうちで朝御飯を（お）食べました

7. I went to America last year.

Watashi 私　= I
Ikimashita 行きました = Went
Amerika アメリカ　= America
Kyonen 去年 = Last year
Wa は, ni に

Answer:
Watashi wa kyonen amerika ni ikimashita.
私は去年アメリカに行きました

Expressing Desire 欲求表現

Knowing how to express what you want is extremely helpful in Japanese.

Nouns are used together with **hoshii 欲しい** when expressing that you want a certain object.

(Watashi wa) noun + ga hoshii desu
(I want... object)

We use ga particle anytime we are stating desires. In this case, it does not state emphasis, it is just one of those patterns we have to accept and shouldn't analyse.

Example sentences:
(Watashi wa) atarashii pasokon ga hoshii desu
私は）新しいパソコンが欲しいです
(Atarashii 新しい= new)
(Pasokon パソコン = PC)
I want a new PC

Kakkoii kareshi ga hoshii desu
かっこいい彼氏が欲しいです
(Kakkoii かっこいい = handsome)

(Kareshi 彼氏 = boyfriend)
I want a handsome boyfriend

Changing **hoshii 欲しい** into its negative form allows is to express that we do not want something.

In Japanese **hoshii 欲しい** is an adjective not a verb. Therefore its conjugation is the same as any i – adjective.

(Watashi wa) noun + ga hoshikunai desu
(I do not want...)

Example sentences:
Takai purezento ga hoshikunai desu
高いプレゼントが欲しいです
(Takai 高い = expensive)
(Purezento プレゼント = present)
I do not want expensive presents

Shukudai ga hoshikunai desu
宿題が欲しくないです
(Shukudai 宿題 = homework)
I do not want homework

Exercise:

Translate the following sentences to Japanese.

1. I want kind friends

(Kind = yasashii 優しい)

(Friends = tomodachi 友達)

Answer:

Yasahii tomodachi ga hoshii desu

優しい友達が欲しいです

2. I want a beautiful haircut

(Beautiful = kirei 綺麗)

(Haircut = kaminoke 髪の毛)

Answer:

Kirei na kaminoke ga hoshii desu

綺麗な髪の毛が欲しいです

3. I do not want noisy neighbors

(Noisy = urusai うるさい)

(Neighbor = rinjin 隣人)

Answer:

Urusai rinjin ga hoshikunai desu.

うるさい隣人が欲しくないです

4. I do not want a slow car

(Slow = osoi 遅い) (Car = kuruma 車)

Answer:
Osoi kuruma ga hoshikunai desu
遅い車が欲しくないです

Want to – Tai Form たい活用形

In the previous section we learnt how to say we want something with "hoshii 欲しい".

If we "want to do something" we cannot use "hoshii 欲しい". Instead we have to use a different form of conjugation, which is tai たい form. Remember "hoshii 欲しい" can only be used with nouns.

hoshii 欲しい = want (for nouns)
tai たい form = want to (verbs)

The easiest way to conjugate into tai form is to start from the masu conjugation. From here the first step is to take off the masu part of the verb.

Example:

Taberu	→	**Tabe**~~masu~~	→**Tabe**
Nomu	→	**Nomi**~~masu~~	→**Nomi**
Kau	→	**Kai**~~masu~~	→**Kai**
Kaku	→	**Kaki**~~masu~~	→**Kaki**
Hanasu	→	**Hanashi**~~masu~~	→**Hanashi**
Iku	→	**Iki**~~masu~~	→**Iki**
Suru	→	**Shi**~~masu~~	→**Shi**
Kuru	→	**Ki**~~masu~~	→**Ki**

Once we have this we add "tai" to the verb.

Example:

Taberu → Tabe → Tabetai
(*ru*-verb)

Nomu → Nomi → Nomitai
(*u*-verb)

Kau → Kai → Kaitai
(*u*-verb)

Kaku → Kaki → Kakitai
(*u*-verb)

Hanasu → Hanashi → Hanashitai
(*u*-verb)

Iku → Iki → Ikitai
(*u*-verb)

Suru → Shi → Shitai
(irregular verb)

Kuru → Ki → Kitai (irregular verb)

When using tai form in polite level speech we need to include desu at the end. Without desu the statement sounds very casual.

When using tai form we can also use particles ga or o. Both are interchangeable.

... + ga/o + verb (tai form) + desu
(I want to do...)

Example sentences:
I want to drink tea
(watashi wa) o-cha ga nomitai desu
(私は）お茶が欲しいです
(tea = o-cha お茶) (drink = nomu)

I want to eat fish
(watashi wa) sakana o tabetai desu
(私は）魚を（お）食べたいです
(fish = sakana 魚) (eat = taberu 食べる)

One thing that confuses many students when we use tai form is the ending. Since tai ends in "I", the verb actually becomes an "I" adjective.

Therefore when we want to make a negative form of this phrase, we have to use i adjective conjugation.

So to conjugation *i-* adjectives into past present, we use kunai.

Example:
Tabetai → **Tabeta**i
→**Tabeta**kunai

Nomitai → **Nomita**i
→**Nomita**kunai

Kaitai → **Kaita**i
→**Kaita**kunai

Kakitai → **Kakita**i
→**Kakita**kunai

Hanashitai → **Hanashita**i
→**Hanashita**kunai

Ikitai → **Ikita**i
→**Ikita**kunai

Shitai → **Shita**i
→**Shita**kunai

Kitai → **Kita**i
→**Kita**kunai

Example sentences:

I don't want to watch that movie

Sono eiga o mitakunai desu

その映画を（お）観たくないです

(movie = eiga 映画) (watch = miru 観る)

I don't want to go to school

Watashi wa gakko ni ikitakunai desu

私は学校に行きたくないです

(school = gakko 学校) (go = iku 行く)

We have to use "ni に" as we are stating direction of movement

Exercise:

Express the desire to do/ to not do something by forming sentences with given words.

1. Shuumatsu + eiga + miru (Positive)

(Shuumatsu = weekend) (Eiga = movie) (Miru = to see, to watch)

Answer:

Shuumatsu ni eiga o/ ga mitai desu

週末に映画を（お）/が観たいです

2. Heya + soji suru (Negative)

(Heya = room) (Soji suru = to clean)

Answer:
Heya o/ ga soji shitakunai desu
部屋を（お）/が掃除したくないです

3. Rainen + Nihon + iku (Positive)
(Rainen = next year) (Nihon = Japan) (Iku = to go)

Answer:
Rainen Nihon ni ikitai desu
来年日本に行きたいです

4. Kono + mise + fuku + kau (Negative)
(Mise = store) (Fuku = clothes) (Kau = to buy)

Answer:
Kono mise de fuku o/ ga kaitakunai desu
この店で服を（お）/が買いたくないです

Frequency Words 頻度を表す単語

Frequency words are very helpful in Japanese, they are used to state how often you do something.
Below are a list of common frequency words:

Always   =   **Itsumo いつも**
Often   =   **Yoku よく**
Usually   =   **Taitei たいてい**
Sometimes =   **Tokidoki ときどき**
Not much   =   **Amari あまり + negative**
Rarely   =   **Mettani 滅多に + negative**
Never   =   **Zenzen 全然 + negative**

Every day   =   **Mainichi 毎日**
Every week   =   **Maishuu 毎週**
Every weekend   =   **Maishuu matsu 毎週末**

These frequency words are usually placed after the topic of the sentence.

Examples:
I often watch a movie
= (Watashi wa) Yoku eiga o mimasu.
(私は）よく映画を（お）観ます
(movie = eiga 映画)

I go to a bar every weekend

= Maishumatsu Baa ni ikimasu

毎週末バーに行きます

(bar = baa バー)

When we use words like "not much", "rarely" "not at all" double negations apply. Therefore they have to be followed by a negative form.

Example:

I do not eat fish at all

= Zenzen sakana o tabemasen

全然魚を（お）食べません

(fish = sakana 魚)

I rarely drink coffee

= Mettani kohi o nomimasen

滅多にコーヒーを（お）飲みません

(coffee = kohi コーヒー)

Inviting お誘い

In this chapter we will cover how to invite someone to do something.

Invitation expressions go as follows:

Why don't we~? /Won't you~?
Verb + present negative masu form + ka?

This pattern is normally used with the word "issho ni 一緒に" which means together.

Examples:
Issho ni ohirugohan o tabemasen ka?
一緒にお昼ご飯を（お）食べませんか
= **Why don't we have lunch together?**
(isshoni 一緒に = together)
(ohirugohan お昼ご飯 = lunch)

Issho ni eiga o mimasen ka?
一緒に映画を（お）観ませんか
= **Why don't we watch a movie together?**
(movie = eiga 映画) (watch = miru 観る)

You can answer in the follow way:
Yes: Hai, ii desu ne.
はい、いいですね

No: Sumimasen, chotto…
すみません、ちょっと…
(sumimasen すみません = sorry)

Japanese people usually don't say "no" when refusing, instead they use "chotto ちょっと". "Chotto ちょっと" literally means "a bit", but it shows your hesitation. The person will understand that you are not able to or you simply don't want to.

Exercise

There are three situations. Read carefully and think about how to invite someone using the given words.

1. You have two movie tickets and want to ask your friend if he/she wants to watch a movie tomorrow.

Movie = Eiga 映画
Watch = Miru 観る
Tommorrow = Ashita 明日

Invite:

Answer:
Ashita eiga o (issho ni) mimasen ka?
明日映画を（お）観ませんか

2. You are going to study Japanese in the library at 5pm today. You want to invite your friends as well.

Study = Benkyosuru 勉強する
Japanese = Nihongo 日本語
Library = Toshokan 図書館

Invite:

Answer:
Kyou, Goji ni toshokan de benkyo shimasen ka?
今日、五時に図書館で勉強しませんか

3. It's lunch time now, but you have no one to eat with you today. Invite someone to your lunch.

Eat = Taberu 食べる
Lunch = Ohirugohan お昼御飯

Together = Isshoni 一緒に

Invite:

Answer:
Isshoni ohirugohan o tabemasen ka?
一緒にお昼御飯を（お）食べませんか

Te-form て―活用形

Te-form can used in a variety of different situations in japanese and is a handy part of Japanese grammar. We will cover its usages in later sections, however first we need to know how to make verbs into te form.

As with all verbs in Japanese, the conjugation will be different depending on the type of verb.

Ru-verbs:
1. Drop the final "ru"
2. Add "te"
   e.g. Taberu (to eat) →   Tabe + te
   →   Tabete

Ru verb usually end in "eru" or iru" however there are some exceptions.

U-verbs:
Using Te-form with u-verbs is more complicated, as these verbs are divided into five categories.

Each is conjugated differently depending on the ending of the verb.

U-verbs with final **u, tsu, ru**:

1. Drop the highlighted part.
2. Add "tte"

e.g. Ka~~u~~ (to buy) →   Ka + tte
→ Katte

e.g. Ma~~tsu~~ (to wait) →   Ma + tte
→ Matte

e.g. Waka~~ru~~ (to understand) →   Waka + tte
→ Wakatte

U-verbs with final **mu, bu, nu**:
1. Drop the highlighted part
2. Add "nde"

e.g. No~~mu~~ (to drink) →   No + nde
→ Nonde

e.g. Aso~~bu~~ (to play) →   Aso + nde
→ Asonde

e.g. Shi~~nu~~ (to die) →   Shi + nde
→ Shinde

U-verbs with final **ku**:
1. Drop the highlighted part
2. Add "ite"

e.g. Ka~~ku~~ (to write) →   Ka + ite
→ Kaite

An exception to this rule is verb **Iku (to go)**, which is conjugated as Itte.

U-verbs with final **gu**:
1. Drop the highlighted part
2. Add "ide"
e.g. Oyogu (to swim) → **Oyo + ide**
→ Oyoide

U-verbs with final **su**:
1. Drop the highlighted part
2. Add "shite"
e.g. Hanasu (to talk) → **Hana + shit**
→ Hanashite

Irregular verbs:
Irregular verbs conjugate as follows:

e.g. Suru (to do) → **Shite**
e.g. Kuru (to come) → **Kite**

A common mistake students make when learning *te*-form is confusing it with the masu form conjugation. Try not to make this mistake, unforntunately te form conjugation is more complicated and we just have to try and memorise it.

Exercise

Practice: Write the following words in *te*-form:

Neru (to sleep)
Au (to meet)
Shinu (to die)
Matsu (to wait)
Miru (to see, to watch)
Wakaru (to understand, u-verb)
Asobu (to play)
Kiku (to ask, to listen)
Yomu (to read)
Oyogu (to swim)
Kasu (to lend)
Benkyo suru (to study)
Kuru (to come)
Iku (to go)
Taberu (to eat)
Sakebu (to scream)
Kiotukeru (to watch out)
Katu (to win)
Kau (to buy)
Kaku (to write)
Shinnjiru (to trust)
Tasukeru (to help)
Kesu (to erase)

Answers

Neru (to sleep) Nete
Au (to meet) Atte
Shinu (to die) Shinde
Matsu (to wait) Matte
Miru (to see, to watch) Mite
Wakaru (to understand, u-verb) Wakatte
Asobu (to play) Asonde
Kiku (to ask, to listen) Kiite
Yomu (to read) Yonde
Oyogu (to swim) Oyoide
Kasu (to lend) Kashite
Benkyo suru (to study) Benkyo shite
Kuru (to come) Kite
Iku (to go) Itte
Taberu (to eat) Tabete
Sakebu (to scream) Sakende
Kiotukeru (to watch out) Kiotukete
Katu (to win) Katte
Kau (to buy) Katte
Kaku (to write) Kaite
Shinnjiru (to trust) Shinjite
Tasukeru (to help) Tasukete
Kesu (to erase) Keshite

Present Continuous Form
現在継続の表し方

Present continuous form is used when describing actions that are ongoing. Such as "I'm eating", "she is driving", "we are going" etc.
There are two ways we use present contionous form.

To make general "-ing" sentences we have to use te form with iru/imasu

Te form + iru/imasu
(...ing)

Iru is used for informal speech and imasu is used for formal speech.

Examples

I am eating (f)
Watashi wa tabette imasu
私は食べています
(to eat = tabemasu)

She is drinking (f)

Kanojo wa nonde imasu
彼女は飲んでいます
(to drink = nomu)

I am reading a book (inf)
Ima hon o yonde iru
今本を読んでいる
(now = ima 今) (to read = yomu 読む)
(book = hon 本)

To make more sentences we can conjugate imasu and iru just like they were any other verb:

Present negative
She is not eating
Kanojo wa tabette imasen
彼女は食べていません (f)
Kanojo wa tabette inai(inf)

Past Postive
She was eating
Kanojo wa tabette imashita (f)
彼女は食べていました
Kanojo wa tabette ita (inf)
彼女は食べていた

Past negative
She was not eating
Kanojo wa tabette imasen deshita (f)
彼女は食べていませんでした

Kanojo wa tabette inakatta (inf)
彼女は食べていなかった

Using "ing" with verbs and adjectives
When we have a "ing" verb and adjective in the same sentence we follow a different pattern.

In this case, the sentence doesn't mean a action that you are doing right now but is instead just talking about the topic.

Examples
Singing is fun
Studying is boring

In these examples we have a "ing" verb and an adjective. Here we cannot use "Te form + iru/imasu", instead we have to use the particle "no の".

The particle "no の" is normally used for possession but as you know, in Japanese particles can have many uses. This is just another use of "no の" particle.

Langauge pattern:

Verb plain form + no + particle + adjective + desu

"desu です" makes this sentence a polite level sentence. We can omit "desu です" to make the sentence casual.

Let's look at some examples

Singing is fun (inf)
Utau no wa tanoshī
歌うのは楽しい
(sing = utau 歌う) (fun = tanoshii 楽しい)

I like studying (f)
Benkyo suru no ga suki desu
勉強するのが好きです
(to study = benkyo suru 勉強する)

I like playing games (f)
Gemu o suru no wa suki desu
ゲームを（お）するのは好きです
(playing games = gemu o suru ゲームを（お）する)

When we use "no" in this way, the "ing" verb actually becomes a noun.

Negative form

To create negative forms of these sentences, we simply have to use the same conjugations in previous sections:

Danicing is not fun
Odoru no wa Tanoshikunai desu
踊るのは楽しくないです

Studying Japanese is not easy (inf)
Nihongo o hanasu no wa kantan ja nai
日本語を（お）話すのは簡単じゃないです

I don't like drinking alchocol
Osake o nomu no wa suki ja nai desu
お酒を（お）飲むのは好きじゃないです

When we conjugate this pattern, we only change the adjective and the verb stays the same.

Exercise:
Translate the following sentences to Japanese.

1. I am watching tv
(tv = terebi テレビ) (watch = miru 見る)

Answer:
Terebi o mite imasu
テレビを（お）見ています

2. The baby is sleeping
(baby = akachan 赤ちゃん) (to sleep = neru 寝る)

Answer:
Akachan wa nete imasu
赤ちゃんは寝ています

3. Recently I have been watching game of thrones
(recently = saikin 最近) (to watch = miru 見る)

Answer:
Saikin game of thrones o mite imasu
最近ゲームオブソローンを（お）見ています

4. She is teaching
(she = kanojo 彼女) (to teach = oshieru 教える)

Answer:
Kanojo wa oshiete imasu
彼女は教えています

5. Singing is not fun
(to sing = utau 歌う) (fun = tanoshii 楽しい)

Answer:
Utau no wa tanoshikunai desu

歌うのは楽しくないです

I Have 私は持っています

When we want to say that we have something, we use the following phrase:

Object ga Arimasu/Imasu

I have object

Arimasu あります is used or non-living things such as a table, a chair or dead animals like fish in a market.

Imasu います is used for living creatures such as a cat, a dog and humans.

Aru ある and iru いる are the informal versions of arimasu / imasu.

Ga is used again here, it does not contain any special meaning but is instead just used in this phrase.

Examples

I have a cat

Neko ga imasu
猫がいます

I have a car

Kuruma ga arimasu
車があります

We can also add the subject to the front of the sentence to state a person has an item.

Person wa object ga imasu/arimasu
Person has object

Example

Mr suki has a cat

Suki san wa neko ga imasu
スキさんは猫がいます
(cat = neko 猫)

Ms Yudi has a younger sister   (inf)

Yudi wa imoto ga iru
ユディは妹がいる
(younger sister = imoto 妹)

To make this into a question we just need to add the particle "ka か" to the end of the sentence.

Mr suki has a cat

Suki san wa neko ga imasu

スキさんは猫がいます

Does Mr suki have a cat?

Suki san wa neko ga imasu ka?

スキさんは猫がいますか

Conjugation of have

The conjugation of imasu and arimasu is the same as any other masu verb.

Present Postive   =   Imasu / arimasu
Present Negative   =   Imasen / arimasen
Past Positive   =   Imashita / arimashita
Past Negative   =   Imasen deshita / arimasen deshita

Examples

Mr suki does not have a cat

Suki san wa neko ga imasen

スキさんは猫がいません

Ms Judai does not have a car
Yudi san wa kuruma ga arimasen
ユディさんは車がありません

However the conjugaton of aru and iru is slightly different

Positive Present	=	aru
Negative Present	=	nai
Positive Past	=	atta
Negative Past	=	nakkata

Positive Present	=	iru
Negative Present	=	inai
Positive Past	=	ita
Negative Past	=	inakatta

Examples
I don't have money
Okane ga nai
お金がない
(money = okane お金)

I didn't have time
Jikan ga nakkatta
時間がなかった
(time = jikan 時間)

I had a cat

Watashi wa neko ga ita
私は猫がいた
(cat = neko 猫)

Exercise

Translate the given sentences:

1. I have a younger brother.

Answer:
Ototo ga imasu.
弟がいます

2. She had a boyfriend.

Answer:
Kanjyo wa kareshi ga imashita.
彼女は彼氏がいました

3. I have no pets.
(pet = petto ペット)

Answer:
Petto ga imasen.
ペットがいません

4. He did not have money.

Answer:

Kare wa okane ga arimasen deshita.
彼はお金がありませんでした

Existence - There is/ There are
存在 - がある

When describing the location/existence of something, we also use imasu/arimasu. However the pattern is slightly different:

Thing + ga + location + ni + arimasu/imasu

We can also use aru/iru for informal speech
Ga particle is always used when talking about existence. We have learnt about particle "ni に" in a previous section. We also use "ni に" when talking about location/existence. "ni に" in these situations translates to "in" or "at"

Let's look at some examples.
Gakko ni sensei ga imasu.
学校に先生がいます
(gakko 学校 =school) (sensei 先生 = teacher)
= There are teachers at a school
At school ….. (gakko ni)

Kyoshitsu ni tsukue to isu ga arimasu.
教室に机と椅子があります

(Kyoshitsu 教室 = classroom) (Tsukue 机 = desk) (Isu 椅子 = chair)

= There are desks and chairs in the classroom.

In the classroom …. (kyoshitsu ni)

Watashi no heya ni terebi ga aru
私の部屋にテレビがある (inf)
(Heya 部屋 = room) (terebi テレビ = TV)

= There is a TV in my room.

In my room …. (watashi no heya ni)

As you can see from these phrase we are talking about the existence of an item therefore we use imasu/arimasu. And since we are talking about where they exist, we have to use particle "ni".

Adding pre-positions

We can also use prepositions words to further explain the location of an item.

List of pre positions

On	Ue 上
In	Naka 中
Under	Shita 下

Front	Mae 前
Behind	Ushiro 後ろ
Next	Yoko 横/Tonari 隣
Near	Chikaku 近く
Between	Aida 間

When combining with a noun, such as "on the table", "next to the school", the preposition phrases go as follows:

Place/object + no + preposition

Examples:

On the desk = Tsukue no ue
机の上

Under the chair = Isu no shita
椅子の下

Near my house = Ie no chikaku
家の近く

Now you know how to say "there is/are" and location words.
We can now put these two phrases together to make a more descriptive sentence:

Place/object + no + pre postion + ni + object + ga + arimasu/imasu

As stated before we need to include the particle "ni に" when talking about location.

Example Sentences:
Tsukue no ue ni enpitsu ga arimasu
机の上に鉛筆があります
(Pencil = Enpitsu 鉛筆), (Desk = Tsukue 机)
= **There is a pencil on the desk.**

Suupaa no tonari ni hanaya ga arimasu
スーパーの隣に花屋があります
(Suupaa スーパー = supermarket)
(hanaya 花屋 = flower shop)
=**There is a flower shop next to the supermarket**

Yoshida san no tonari ni watashi ga iru (inf)
吉田さんの隣に私がいる
= **Yoshida is next to me**

Asking for location of an item

When you want to know the location of an object, you can use the question word "where どこ" (doko). We can use this with arimasu/imasu. The sentence structure goes as follows:

Doko + ni + object + ga + arimasu/imasu + ka?
Where is (object)?

Where is the pencil?
= Doko ni enpitsu ga arimasu ka?
どこに鉛筆がありますか

In the pencase.
= Fudebako no naka ni arimasu.
筆箱の中にあります
(Pencase = Fudebako 筆箱)

Exercise
Translate the following sentences.

1. There is a flower shop in front of the station.
(Flower shop = Hanaya 花屋), (Station = Eki 駅)

Answer:
Eki no mae ni hanaya ga arimasu.
駅の前に花屋があります

2. There is a cat under the chair.

(Cat = Neko 中), (Chair = Isu 椅子)

Answer:

Isu no shita ni eko ga imasu.
椅子の下に猫がいます

3. There is a dog next to the man (inf)

(man = o toko 男), (next to = tonari 隣), (Dog = Inu 犬)

Answer:

O toko no tonari ni inu ga iru.
男の隣に犬がいる

Making Requests 依頼

Since we have learnt te-form, we can now start putting it to use. Te-form can be used together with **kudasai** ください, in order to make a polite request to another person.

Verb *te*-form + kudasai
(please do …)

Example:

Oshie<u>ru</u>	→	Oshie<u>te</u> kudasai
No<u>mu</u>	→	No<u>nde</u> kudasai
Ka<u>ku</u>	→	Ka<u>ite</u> kudasai
Hana<u>su</u>	→	Hana<u>shite</u> kudasai
I<u>ku</u>	→	I<u>tte</u> kudasai

Example sentences:
Please drink this medicine.
(Kusuri 薬 = medicine) (drink = nomu 飲む)
= **Kono kusuri o** nonde kudasai.
この薬を（お）飲んでください

Please speak in Japanese.
(Nihongo 日本語 = Japanese)
= **Nihongo de** hanashite kudasai.
日本語で話してください

When talking to a close friend or a relative, you can make a less formal request by omitting **kudasai** ください.

Example sentences:
Turn on the TV.
(Tsukeru つける = turn on)
Terebi o tsukete.
テレビを（お）つけて

Do the homework.
(Shukudai 宿題 = homework) (do = suru する)
Shukudai o shite.
宿題を（お）して

Exercise:
Translate the following requests to Japanese.
1. Please eat the vegetables.
(Vegetables = yasai 野菜)

Answer:
Yasai o tabete kudasai.
野菜を（お）ください

2. Please help your parents.
(Parents = ryoshin 両親) (To help = tetsudau 手伝う)

Answer:

Ryoshin o tetsudatte kudasai.
両親を（お）手伝ってください

3. Open the window (inf)

(Window = mado 窓) (To open = akeru 開ける)

Answer:

Mado o akete.
窓を（お）開けて

4. Play with your friends outside (inf)

(To play = asobu 遊ぶ) (Friends = tomodachi 友達) (Outside = soto 外)

Answer:

Tomodachi to soto de asonde.
友達と外で遊ぶ

Asking For Permission 許可を得る

When asking for permission we also use Te-form. We put this together with "mo ii desu ka?"

Verb *te*-form + mo ii desu ka?
(may I do ...?)

Example:

Mi<u>ru</u> → **Mi<u>te</u> mo ii desu ka**
May I watch?
(Miru 見る/観る = to see, to watch)

Hana<u>su</u> → **Hana<u>shite</u> mo ii desu ka**
May I talk?
(Hanasu 話す = to talk)

In casual speech we omit the particles and just leave the verb, "ii" and use a rising tone.

Verb te form + ii + rising tone? (inf)
(may I ... ?)

Examples
Can I sit next to you?
Tonari suwatte ii?
隣座っていい

(next to = tonari 隣) (sit = suwaru 座る)

Can I open the window?
Mado, akete ii?
窓、開けていい
(window = mado 窓) (open = akeru 開ける)

To give our response, we use the te form and "mo ii desu" to say you may. And we use "wa ikemasen" to say you may not.

Verb *te*-form + mo ii desu
(you may do ...)

Verb *te*-form + wa ikemasen
(you may/must not do ...)

Example:
Mi<u>ru</u> → **Mi<u>te</u> mo ii desu**
You may watch
(Miru 見る/観る = to see, to watch)

Hana<u>su</u> → **Hana<u>shite</u> wa ikemasen**
You may not talk
(Hanasu 話す = to talk)

Example sentences:

A: **Uchi ni kaette mo ii desu ka?**
うちに帰ってもいいですか
(Uchi うち = home)
(Kaeru 帰る = to go home, return)
May I go home?

B: **Hai, kaette mo ii desu.**
はい、帰ってもいいです
Yes, you may.

A: **Shashin wo totte mo ii desu ka?**
写真を撮ってもいいですか
(Shashin 写真 = picture) (Toru 撮る = to take)
May I take a picture?

B: **Koko de shashin o totte wa ikemasen.**
ここで写真を撮ってはいけません
You must not take a picture here.

Exercise:
Ask for permission by forming sentences with given words.

1. Jitensha + kariru
(Jitensha 自転車 = bicycle)
(Kariru 借りる = to borrow)

Answer:

Jitensha o karite mo ii desu ka?
自転車を借りてもいいですか

2. Atarashii + kutsu + kau

(Atarashii 新しい= new) (Kutsu 靴= shoes) (Kau 買う = to buy)

Answer:

Atarashii kutsu o katte mo ii desu ka?
新しい靴を（お）買ってもいいですか

3. Denwa + hanasu

(Denwa 電話= telephone)
(Hanasu 話す= to speak)

Answer:

Denwa de hanashite mo ii desu ka?
電話で話してもいいですか

Expressing too much 過剰表現

When we want to express "too" in a sentence we use the word "sugiru すぎる". We place this after the verb or adjective we are talking about. In order to use this in a sentence we need to conjugate.

Language pattern

       Adjective/verb + sugiru/sugimasu

Sugiru is used for informal speech
Sugimasu is used for formal speech

Let's look at using sugiru with adjectives first:

I adjectives with sugiru
We have to remove the final I and add sigiru.
I adjective (remove final i) + sigiru

Na adjectives with sigiru
We remove the final na and add sigiru:
Na adjective (remove na) + sigiru

Let's see some examples

Too expensive

= takasugiru 高すぎる (inf)
= takasugimasu 高すぎます (f)
(expensive = takai 高い)

Too cold
= samusugru 寒すぎる (inf)
= samusugimasu 寒すぎます (f)
(cold = samui 寒い)

Too quiet
= Shizuka sugiru 静かすぎる (inf)
= Shizuka sugimasu 静かすぎます (f)
(quiet = shizuka na 静かな)

Examples in full sentences

This watch is too expensive
Kono tokei wa takasugirimasu
この時計は高すぎます
(expensive = takai 高い)

This library is too quiet
Kono toshoukan wa shizuka sugimasu
この図書館は静かすぎます
(quiet = shizuka na 静かな)

This new job is too hard
Atarashi shigoto wa taihen sugiru
新しい仕事は大変すぎる
(hard = taihen na 大変な)

Negations are the same as any other verb, therefore we can conjugate in the following way:

Present Positive
=	Takasugimasu / sugiru
Present Negative
=	Takasugimasen / sugi nai
Past Positive
=	Takasugimashita / sugita
Past Negative
=	Takasugimasen deshita / suginakatta

Sugiru with verbs
When using sigiru with verbs ending in "iru" and "eru" we have to chop off the final ru and add sigiru

Misugiru 見すぎる

To watch too much
(watch = miru)

Tabesugiru 食べすぎる

To watch too much
(eat = taberu)

Nesugiru 寝すぎる

To sleep too much
(sleep = neru)

Example sentences
I slept too much yesterday (inf)
Kinō wa nesugita
昨日は寝すぎた

My little brother always watches too much TV (f)
Otōto wa itsumo terebi o misugimasu
弟はいつもテレビを（お）見すぎます

Sugiru with u verbs
For all other verbs ending in u, take off the 'u' and add sigiru.

Drank too much
Nomisugiru 飲みすぎる
(drink = nomu)

Wrote too much
Kakisugita 書きすぎる
(kaku = write)

Don't get confused!
If you're talking about "too" as in "me too /as well", here you have to use "mo も" particle and not sigiru すぎる.

I like sushi
Watashi mo sushi ga suki desu
私も寿司が好きです
(I as well like sushi)

Exercise
Translate the given sentences:
1. This pen is too cheap.
(cheap = yasui 安い)

Answer:

Kono pen wa yasusugimasu.
このペンは安すぎます

2. She worked too much yesterday.

Answer:

Kanjyo wa kinou shigoto sisugimashita.
彼女は昨日仕事しすぎました

Counters 数え方

Japanese does not have plural form. Instead we use counter to state the amount of an item.

In English when to count something we can simply say what it is.
1 pen, 2 photos. 3 people

However in Japanese certain objects have their own specific counters
1 pen = ippon 一本
2 photos = nimai 二枚
3 people = sannin 三人

There are tons of counters in Japanese. But don't worry, you don't have to learn all of them to use counters.

Let's go through some common ones

Nin 人 counter
For counting people we use the "nin 人" counter. The first two have special names but the rest follow the pattern "nin 人"

1 person	=	Hitori 一人
2 people	=	Futari 二人

3 people = Sanin 三人
4 people = Yonin 四人
5 people = Gonin 五人
6 people = Rokunin 六人
7 people = Shichinin 七人
8 people = Hachinin 八人
9 people = Kyuunin 九人
10 people = Juunin 十人
100 people = Hyakunin 百人
1000 people = Sennin 千人
How many people = Nannin? 何人

Ko 個 counter

Ko 個 can be used to count small objects, such as apples, eggs etc. We simply add ko 個 to the number.

1 = Iko 一個
2 = Niko 二個
3 = Sanko 三個
4 = Yonko 四個
5 = Goko 五個
6 = Rokko 六個
7 = Nanako 七個
8 = Hakko 八個
9 = Kyuuko 九個
10 = Juko 十個
100 = hyakko 百個
1000 = senko 千個

How many = nanko? 何個

Generic counter
This counter can be used for counting generic things, like icecream, keys, chairs etc. These counters only go up to 10.

1 = Hitotsu 一つ
2 = Futatsu 二つ
3 = Mittsu 三つ
4 = Yottsu 四つ
5 = Itsutsu 五つ
6 = Muttsu 六つ
7 = Nanatsu 七つ
8 = Yattsu 八つ
9 = Kokonotsu 九つ
10 = Too 十
How many = Ikutsu いくつ

After 10 you can use ko 個 counter to count more.

Ordering 注文

Now that we have learnt about counters, we can learn how to order in Japanese. We use the words "onegaishimasu お願いします" and "kudasai ください" when placing an order.

Onegaishimasu and kudasai both translate to "please", however onegaishimasu is more polite.

> …. Onegaishimasu / kudasai
> … please

Examples

A vegetable ramen and a beer please

Yasai ramen to bīru kudasai

野菜ラーメンとビールください

(vegetable = yasai 野菜)

Can I have a menu please?

Menu onegaishimasu

メニューお願いします

When ordering more than one of something, we need to use counters. The best way to do this is by using the following language pattern:

Food/drink name + (number + ko /tsu counter) + kudasai

Example

Can I have four waters please

Mizu o yonko kudasai
水を（お）四個ください
or
Mizu o yotsu kudasai
水を（お）四つください
(water = mizu 水)

Can I have 3 beer and 2 salmon please

Biru o mitsu to sāmon o futatsu kudasai
ビールを（お）三つとサーモンを（お）二つください
or
Biru o sanko to sāmon o niko kudasai
ビールを（お）三個とサーモンを（お）二個ください
(beer = biru ビール)

Sometimes when ordering you might not know the name of the items you want. In this case we can use the word "kore これ" and simply point out the items off the menu.

I want this and this please

Kore to kore o kudasai
これとこれを（お）ください

A few common phrases you may here

When entering the restaurant you will hear, "Irasshaimase". This means "welcome" and used to greet customers.

Next you'll be asked "nan nin desu ka 何人ですか?" which translates to "how many people?" We can answer this with the number of people plus the people counter "nin"

3 people =   sannin desu 三人です
2 people =   futari desu 二人です

Finally when you want to call the waiter to "ask for the bill" or "to order" you can use the following phrases:

Excuse me
Sumimasen
すみません

Order please
Chumon onegaishimasu
注文お願いします
(order = chumon 注文)

Check please

Okaikei onegaishimasu
お会計お願いします

(cheque = okaikei お会計)

Exercise

Translate the given sentences:

1. Excuse me, can I have a menu please?

Answer:

Sumimasen, menu onegaishimasu.
すみません、メニューお願いします

2. Miso ramen and two beer please.

Answer:

Miso ramen to biru hutatu kudasai.
味噌ラーメンとビール二つください

3. Check please. And can I have 10 water please?

(And = soreto それと)

Answer:

Okaikei onegaishimasu. Soreto, mizu o too kudasai.
お会計お願いします。あと、水を（お）十ください

Masho – let's ましょう

When we want to suggest to do something we use the word "masho". This translates to "let's".

Lets ……
…. Masho

To use this we simply have to take the masu part off a verb and replace it with masho.

Examples
Let's eat dinner
Bangohan o tabemasho
晩御飯を（お）食べましょう
(dinner = bangohan 晩御飯)

Lets see a movie together
Issho ni eiga o mimasho
一緒に映画を（お）観ましょう
(together = issho ni 一緒に)

Lets study Japanese
Nihongo o benkyo shimasho
日本語を（お）勉強しましょう
(Japanese language = nihongo 日本語)

Lets study at the library

Toshokan ni benkyo shimasho
図書館に勉強しましょう
(library = toshokan 図書館)

Using "let's" informally
Making "let's" sentences in informal tense can be trickier. The conjugation is slightly different depending on the verb endings.

For verbs that have "iru" and "eru" ending, we change the last "ru" to "you".

Examples
Let's eat (inf)
Tabeyo 食べよう

Let's eat lunch here (inf)
Koko de hirugohan o tabeyou
ここで昼ご飯を（お）食べよう

Let's sleep (inf)
Neyou 寝よう

For all other u verb endings, we change the u into ou

To go (inf)
Iku = ikou 行こう

Let's go to japan (inf)
Nihon ni ikou
日本に行こう

Let's drink tea (inf)
Ochaa o nomou
お茶を（お）飲もう

For the two irregular verbs, they conjugate in the following way:
Suru =   shiyou しよう
Kuru =   koyou 来よう

Exercise
Translate the given sentences:
1. Let's go to the restaurant together.

Answer:
Issyo ni sono resutoranto ni ikimasyo.
一緒にそのレストランに行きましょう

2. Let's discuss about it.
(discuss = hanashiau 話し合う)
(about = ni tuite について)

Answer:
Sore ni tuite hanashiaimasyo.

それについて話し合いましょう

3. Let's eat lunch together. (inf)

Answer:
Issyo ni hirugohan o tabemasyo.
一緒に昼ご飯を（お）食べましょう

More than 比較級—より

In this section we are going to learn how to compare things together, for example A is better than B. To make these sentences, we use "ho ga" and "yori".
The language pattern goes as follows

A no hoga B yori C desu
A is C than B

No hoga = is more
Yori = than
C = verb or adjective you are comparing

Example
Ramen is better than pasta
Ramen no hoga pasta yori ii desu
ラーメンの方がパスタよりいいです

Snow is better than rain
Yuki no hoga ame yori ii desu
雪の方が雨よりいいです
(snow = yuki 雪) (rain = ame 雨)

When C is an adjective we don't have to conjugate. Literally translated this sentence means "ramen is good than pasta". However in Japanese "better" is translated as "good". Therefore we use the word "ii いい" in this situation.

We can also change C to a different adjective, to create other comparative sentences.

Example
Sam is smarter than dave
Sam no ho ga dave yori atama ga ii desu
サムの方がデイブより頭がいいです
(smart = atama ga ii 頭がいい)

Hanako is cooler/handsome than Hiroko
Hanako no hoga Hiroko yori kakkoi desu
花子のほうが弘子よりかっこいいです
(cooler/handsome = kakkoi かっこいい)

I like vegetables better than meat
Yasai no hoga niku yori suki desu
野菜の方が肉より好きです
(vegetables = yasai 野菜) (meat = niku 肉)

What confuses most beginners, is that we can actually change the order of the sentence. However the meaning remains the same:

B yori A no hoga C desu
Than B, A is (adjective)

Example
Snow is better than rain
Ame yori yuki no hoga ii desu
雨より雪のほうがいい
Than rain, snow is better

This can be confusing to see, but just remember the meaning is still the same.

To ask someone which one they prefer, we use the following structure

Which one do you prefer A or B?
A to B to dochi no hoga suki (desu ka?)
(dochira is used for formal speech, instead of dochi)

To answer we use the same pattern as before:
I like A more than B
A no hoga b yori suki desu

If we want to say that we like both we can say this in three ways:
I like both

A mo B mo suki desu

Or

Dochi mo suki
どっちも好き
By adding mo, dochi どっち now means both
Dochiramo どちらも is more formal

Or
We can put both together
A mo b mo dochi mo suki (inf)
A mo b mo dochira mo suki desu (f)

One thing to keep in mind, is when we are asking which one you prefer, you can only use dochi どっち and dochira どちら for 2 option. If we have more than two option we use dore どれ "which one" however this is a more advanced level pattern.

Let's see some more comparative examples
Which you prefer summer or winter?
Natsu to fuyu to dochi no hoga suki
夏と冬とどちらの方が好き
(summer = natsu 夏) (winter = fuyu 冬)

I prefer dogs to cats
Watashi wa inu no hoga neko yori suki desu
私は犬の方が猫より好きです

(dog = inu 犬) (cat = neko 猫)

Kfc is a little bit more expensive than mcdonalds
Kfc no hoga Mc'donalds yori chotto takai desu
ケー・エフ・シーの方がマクドナルドよりちょっと高いです
(little bit = chotto ちょっと)

Exercise
Translate the given sentences:

1. Which do you prefer, beach or mountain? Mountain is better than beach.
(beach = biichi ビーチ) (mountain = yama 山)

Answer:
Biichi to yama dochira no hoga suki desu ka?
Yama no houga biichi yori suki desu.
ビーチと山どちらの方が好きですか？山の方がビーチよりも好きです

2. Which do you prefer, coffee or tea? I like both. (inf)

Answer:
Koohii to ocha dochi ga suki? Dochi mo suki.
コーヒーとお茶どっちが好き？どっちも好き

3. British English is cooler than American English.

Answer:
Igirisu eigo no hoga amerika eigo yori kakkoii desu.
イギリス英語の方がアメリカ英語よりかっこいいです

The Most 最上級

We have learnt how to compare two things, but how do we say something is the most of something. For this we use the word "ichiban 一番" which translates to "number one". With this we can makes words like, fastest, cutest, longest etc.

Language pattern:

> Ichiban + adjective
> ….. st

Ichiban 一番 = number one

Let's see some examples
The cutest (literally cute no 1)
Ichiban kawaii
一番かわいい

The cutest pokemon is pickaku
Ichiban kawaii pokemon wa pickaku desu
一番かわいいポケモンはピカチュウです
(cute = kawaii かわいい)

Yuki is the most beautiful person (no 1 beautiful person)

Ichiban kirei na hito wa yuki san desu
一番綺麗な人はゆきさんです
(beautiful = kirei na 綺麗な)

Titanic is the saddest movie
Ichiban kanashi eiga wa Titanic desu
一番悲しい映画はタイタニックです
(sad = kanashi 悲しい)

Exercise

Translate the given sentences:

1. Mt. Fuji is the most famous mountain in Japan.

(Mt. Fuji = fujisan 富士山)

Answer:
Nihon de ichiban yumei na yama wa fujisan desu.
日本で一番有名な山は富士山です

2. The most beautiful landscape is Japanese Alps.

(landscape = keshiki 景色)

Answer:
Ichiban kireina keshiki wa nihon alps desu.
一番綺麗な景色は日本アルプスです

3. Yoko is the kindest person.

(kind = yasashi 優しい) (person= hito 人)

Answer:
Ichiban yasashi hito wa yoko desu.
一番優しい人は洋子です

Have you ever?—ことがありますか

To state things that we have done or never dpne, we use the following language pattern:

..ta koto ga aru/arimasu
I have .. (the experience)

This often gets confused with the conjugation of verbs, let's look at the difference:

I went to japan
Nihon ni ikimashita
日本に行きました
(to go = iku 行く)

I have been to japan
Nihon ni ita koto ga arimasu
日本に行ったことがありますか

So we used this phrase to state experiences we have had or we haven't had. TO make the negative form, we conjugate aru to nai and arimasu to arimasen.

Examples
I have never been to japan

Nihon ni ita koto ga nai (inf)
日本に行ったことがない

or

Nihon ni ita koto ga arimasen (f)
日本に行ったことがありません

Have you listened to this?

Kore o kita koto ga arimasu ka?
これを（お）聞いたことがありますか
(listen = kiku 聞く)

I have never listened to it

Kita koto ga arimasen
聞いたことがありません

We can even simplify to say yes or no with aru/arimasu.

Have you listened to this?

Kore o kita koto ga arimasu ka?
これを（お）聞いたことがありますか

Yes

Hai arimasu / aru
はい、あります/ある

No

iee arimasen / nai
いいえ、ありません/ない

Exercise

Translate the given sentences:

1. Have you ever eaten ramen? No I have never eaten ramen.

Answer:

Ramen o tabeta koto ga arimasu ka? Iie ramen o tabeta koto ga arimasen.
ラーメンを（お）食べたことがありますか？いいえ、ラーメンを（お）食べたことがありません

2. Have you ever climbed the mountain? Yes I have.

(to climb = noboru 登る)

Answer:

Sono yama ni nobotta koto ga arimasu ka? Hai arimasu.
その山に登ったことがありますか？はい、あります

3. I have never played the game. (Inf)

Answer:

Sono geemu o shita koto ga nai.
そのゲームを（お）したことがない

Connecting Verbs 動詞のつなぎ方

Previously in the book it was explained that *'to'* particle can connect two nouns, however it cannot be used with verbs.

Te-form is used to connect two or more verbs in order to describe a sequence of actions.
We only use te form to conjugate the first verb, the final verb is left in the tense you want to state (past, present, future).

Example sentences:
Shukudai o shite, yasumimasu.
宿題を（お）して、休みます
(Shukudai 宿題= homework) (Suru する = to do)
(Yasumu 休む = to rest)
I will do my homework and then rest.

Oishii hirugohan wo tabete, gakko ni ikimashita.
おいしい昼ご飯を（お）食べて、学校に行きました
(Oishii おいしい= delicious) (Hirugohan 昼ご飯= breakfast) (Taberu 食べる= to eat)
(Gakko 学校= school) (Iku 行く = to go)
I ate delicious breakfast and went to school.

Suupaa ni itte, kaimono o shimasho.

スーパーに行って、買い物を（お）しましょう

(Suupaa スーパー = supermarket) (Iku 行く = to go) (Kaimono suru 買い物する = to do shopping)
Let's go to the supermarket and do shopping.

Exercise:
Translate the given sentences:
1. I will work and then go back home.

Answer:
Hataraite ie ni kaerimasu.
働いて、家に帰ります

2. We will go to hot spring and then take a rest.
(hot spring = onsen 温泉)

Answer:
Watashitachi wa onsen ni itte yasumimasu.
私達は温泉に行って休みます

3. She will meet her friends and then go shopping.

Answer:
Kanojyo wa tomodachi ni atte kaimono o shimasu.
彼女は友達に会って、買い物を（お）します

Connecting Adjectives
形容詞のつなぎ方

Te – form can also be used to connect two or more adjectives, creating more descriptive sentences. In order to do that, we must learn how to transform adjectives into *te* – form.

I-adjectives:
1. Drop the final "i"
2. Add "kute"

e.g. Kawaii (cute) →   Kawai + kute → Kawaikute.

This also applies to the irregular adjective ii.

Ii (good)   →   Yo + kute   → Yokute.

Na-adjectives:
1. Drop the "na"
2. Add "de"

e.g. Kirei na (beautiful)   →   Kirei + de → Kirei de

When connecting adjectives, the last adjective in the sequence remains normal and is not placed in te form.

Example sentences:
Piza wa yasukute, oishii desu
ピザは安くて、おいしいです
(Piza ピザ = pizza) (Yasui 安い = cheap)
(Oishii おいしい = tasty)
The pizza is cheap and tasty

Tomodachi wa atama ga yokute, genki desu
友達は頭がよくて、元気です
(Tomodachi 友達 = friend) (Atama ga ii 頭がいい = Smart) (Genki 元気 = cheerful)
My friend is smart and cheerful

Kyou wa hima de, taikutsu desu
今日は暇で、退屈です
(Kyou 今日 = today) (Hima 暇 = free)
(Taikutsu 退屈 = boring)
Today is free and boring

Exercise:
Connect the nouns and adjectives to form sentences
1. Tea + sweet + tasty
(Tea お茶 = ocha) (Sweet 甘い = amai)
(Tasty おいしい = oishii)

Answer:
Ocha wa amakute, oishii desu.

お茶は甘くて、おいしいです

2. Puppy + small + cute

(Puppy = koinu 子犬) (Small = chiisai 小さい) (Cute = kawaii かわいい)

Answer:
Koinu wa chiisakute, kawaii desu.
子犬は小さくて、かわいいです

3. Teacher + serious + strict

(Teacher = sensei 先生) (Serious = majime na まじめな) (Strict = kibishii 厳しい)

Answer:
Sensei wa majime de, kibishii desu.
先生はまじめで、厳しいです

4. Boyfriend + kind + handsome + wonderful + person

(Boyfriend = kareshi 彼氏) (Kind = yasashii 優しい) (Handsome = kakkoii かっこいい)
(Wonderful = suteki na 素敵な)
(Person = hito 人)

Answer:
Kareshi wa yasashikute, kakkoyokute, suteki na hito desu.

彼氏は優しくて、かっこよくて、素敵な人です

Telling Time in Japanese
日本語での時間の伝え方

In Japanese, both 12-hour and 24-hour clocks are used, however, 12-hour clock is more common in conversation.

Hour: Ji 時
Minute: Hun, pun 分

To tell time you just need to add "ji 時" to the hour and "hun/pun 分" to the minute. As you know 4, 7, 9 have two forms however we only use a certain type when talking about time:

Hours
4:00 Yo ji 四時
7:00 Shichi ji 七時
9:00 Ku ji 九時

Minutes
1 minute Ippun 一分
2 minutes Nihun 二分
3 minutes Sanpun 三分
4 minutes Yonhun 四分
5 minutes Gohun 五分

6 minutes Roppun 六分
7 minutes   Nanahun 七分
8 minutes Happun 八分
9 minutes Kyuu hun 九分
10 minutes   Juppun 十分
...

The sentence order is the same as English. First we state the hour and then the minutes:

Example
2:15
Niji ju-go hun 二時十五分

We can also use the following phrases to state am and pm:

Am = Gozen 午前
Pm = Gogo 午後

In Japanese AM/PM come in front of the time.

Examples
3:01pm
Gogo sanji ippun 午後三時一分

8:00am
Gozen hatchiji 午前八時

Finally to ask the time we can use the question word:

Nanji? 何時 = what time?

We use this in the set phrase:

What time is it now?
Ima nanji desu ka? 今何時ですか
(now = ima 今)

When talking about minutes we can also use the phrase "han 半" to say half past

3:30
Sanji han 三時半

1:30
Ichiji han 一時半

Exercise
Translate the given sentences:
1.What time is it now? It is 8:20 am.

Answer:
Ima nanji desu ka? Gozen hachiji nijuppunn desu.
今何時ですか？午前八時二十分です

2. What time is it now? It Is 7:30 pm. (Inf)

Answer:

Ima nanji? Gogo shichi ji han.
今何時？午後七時半

3. 9:41 am.

Answer:

Gozen kuji yonju ippun.
午前九時四十一分

Time & Distance 時間と距離

In this section, we will learn asking and answering how much time it takes to get from one place to another.

Question word **dono gurai** どのぐらい (how much) is used when asking how much time it takes to travel a certain distance.

A kara B made dono gurai kakarimasu ka?
How long does it take to get from A to B?
(Kara から = from) (Made まで = to)
(Kakaru かかる = to take /time to do something)

Example:
How long does it take to get from the classroom to the library?
Kyoshitsu kara toshokan made dono gurai kakarimasu ka?
教室から図書館までどのぐらいかかりますか
(Kyoshitsu 教室 = classroom)
(Toshokan 図書館 = Library)

Gurai means 'approximately' or 'about'. When answering a **dono gurai** question you are expected to name an approximate time duration.

A kara B made + time + gurai kakarimasu
(It takes about + time + to get from A to B)

Example:
It takes about 5 minutes to get from the classroom to the library
Kyoshitsu kara toshokan made gofun gurai kakarimasu
教室から図書館まで五分ぐらいかかります
(Kyoshitsu 教室 = classroom) (Toshokan 図書館 = library) (Go-fun 五分 = 5 minutes)
Or simplified
Gofun gurai kakarimasu
五分ぐらいかかります

When you want to get a more precise answer you may ask how many minutes/ hours/ days it takes to get from one place to another. In that case nan + time unit is used in a question instead of dono.

A kara B made nanjikan gurai kakarimasu ka?
(How many hours does it take to get from A to B?)
(hour = jikan 時間)

Example:
How many minutes does it take to get from the station to your home?

Eki kara uchi made nanpun gurai kakarimasu ka?
駅からうちまで何分ぐらいかかりますか
(eki 駅 = station) (uchi うち = home) (nanpun 何分 = how many minutes)

When you want to answer with an exact time duration you can omit gurai:

A kara B made + time + kakarimasu
(It takes + time + to get from A to B)

Example:
It takes 30 minutes
Eki kara uchi made sanjuppun kakarimasu
駅からうちまで三十分かかります
(Eki 駅 = station) (Uchi うち = home)
(Sanjuppun 三十分 = 30 minutes)
Or simplified
Sanjuppun kakarimasu
三十分かかります

Exercise:
Fill in the blank spaces.
1. A: Basutei kara _____ made gurai kakarimasu ka?

B:_____kara suupaa_____ juppun gurai_____.

(Basutei バス停 = bus stop) (Suupaa スーパー = supermarket) (Juppun 十分 = 10 minutes)

Answer:
A: Basutei kara suupaa made dono gurai kakarimasu ka?
バス停からスーパーまでどのぐらいかかりますか
B: Basutei kara suupaa made juppun gurai kakarimasu.
バス停からスーパーまで十分ぐらいかかります

2. A: Tokyo kara_____made nanjikan_____ _____kakarimasu__.
B: _____Kyoto made nijikan gurai kakarimasu.

(Nanjikan 何時間= how many hours)
(Nijikan 二時間= 2 hours)

Answer:

A:

Tokyo kara Kyoto made nanjikan gurai kakarimasu ka?

東京から京都まで何時間ぐらいかかりますか

B:

Tokyo kara Kyoto made nijikan gurai kakarimasu.

東京から京都まで二時間ぐらいかかります

3. A: Apaato kara_____made nanpun _____ka?

    B: Apaato_____konbini_____happun kakarimasu.

    (Apaato アパート = apartment) (Konbini コンビニ = convenience store) (Nanpun 何分 = how many minutes) (Happun 八分 = 8 minutes)

Answer:

A:

Apaato kara konbini made nanfun guraikakarimasu ka?

アパートからコンビニまで何分ぐらいかかりますか

B:
Apaato kara konbini made happun kakarimasu.
アパートからコンビニまで八分かかります

Conclusion

And there you have it, we've reached the end of our Japanese Grammar 101 book.

Congratulations, if you have studied this book thoroughly your grammar will have skyrocketed – not to mention your confidence too. Just think how far you've come. That's amazing progress.

Now you have a solid foundation which you can build on. All you need to do is combine this knowledge with new vocabulary and some practice, then before you know it, your fluency will be through the roof.

I am happy to have helped you along your journey in Japanese and hope we'll talk again soon, definitely in another book.

Never give up on your language goals, with the right resources fluency is just around the corner.

Can I ask a quick favor?

Would you be kind enough to leave a small review for this book on Amazon? I love hearing feedback from you guys.

Thanks for reading our content.
Good luck with your Japanese studies. We'll speak again soon!

Languages World

Made in the USA
Coppell, TX
12 March 2020